DAVID SHIBLEY & JONATHAN SHIBLEY

Marketplace
Memos

Marketplace
Memos

RE: Invest yourself
in the Business of
God's Kingdom

First printing: September 2008

ISBN-13: 978-0-89221-678-9
ISBN-10: 0-89221-678-6
Library of Congress Catalog Number: 2008935705

Unless otherwise noted, all Scripture is from the New King James Version of the Bible, copyright © 1982 by Thomas Nelson, Inc. Used by permission. All rights reserved.

Scripture quotations marked NIV are from the Holy Bible, New International Version, copyright © 1973, 1978, 1984 International Bible Society. Used by permission of Zondervan. All rights reserved.

Scripture quotations marked NLT are from the Holy Bible, New Living Translation, copyright 1996, 2004. Used by permission of Tyndale House Publishers, Inc., Wheaton, Illinois 60189. All rights reserved.

Scripture quotations marked NASB are from the Holy Bible, New American Standard Bible®, copyright © 1960, 1962, 1963, 1968, 1971, 1972,1973, 1975, 1977, 1995 by The Lockman Foundation. Used by permission.

Cover and interior design by Diana Bogardus and Rebekah Krall

Printed in the United States of America

Please visit our website for other great titles:
www.newleafpress.net

For information regarding author interviews, please contact the publicity department at (870) 438-5288.

New Leaf Press
A Division of New Leaf Publishing Group

Contents

Part III
LEAVING A LEGACY
For Christ, His Commission, and His Kingdom

Introduction

*I*n an article for *Fortune* magazine, Marc Gunther wrote, "Marketplace pressures frequently bump up against spiritual values, as businesspeople tackle questions that reverberate beyond the bottom line: How to handle layoffs. How much to pay people. How to reach out to others in a loving way. How to react to unethical conduct. How to make money — of course — and make meaning too."[1]

In *Marketplace Memos,* we address those frequent times and situations when marketplace pressures bump up against spiritual values.

While He was here on earth, Jesus' preferred platform for displaying His power and glory was the marketplace. When it came to ministry and miracles, Jesus clearly preferred the public square to the cloistered confines of the temple. The gamut of today's marketplace is simply the composite of arenas where humans interact. Some refer to these arenas as "seven mountains" that must be scaled and the flag of Christ's Kingdom planted at the summit in order to redemptively transform all of culture. These "mountains" are education, the arts, media, government, the family, religion (or faith), and business. Together these seven spheres mold society, shape belief systems, and house the keys to the global spiritual harvest.

Jesus remains actively at work in the marketplace today. Now, as then, He is "overturning the tables" of greed, lifting the broken, and prospering those who align their values with His. In short, He claims His rightful place as Lord over all of work and life.

Marketplace Memos attacks the unscriptural notion of a truncated life where faith is neatly tucked into one compartment and vocation into another. Although this is often touted as the norm today, such a dichotomized life is also a prescription for spiritual schizophrenia. Jesus must be the CEO and integrator of *all* of life.

Over the last several years, God has spotlighted marketplace ministry. The purpose of this book is to give quick encouragement, biblical principles, and practical insights to Christians who want to be "Kingdom catalysts" in the marketplace. Each memo addresses a practical theme, especially for businesspersons. The section at the end of each memo gives a Scripture for meditation throughout the day, a maxim for reflection, a guide for prayer, and a call to action.

To get the most out of this book, we encourage you to read these pages with:

- *A prayerful heart.* Ask God to equip you to serve honorably as His ambassador in your sphere of influence. Your vocation can be and should be your calling, as well.
- *An open Bible.* Several verses from God's Word are interlaced through each memo. These are annotated, providing you the option of a quick read of the memo with opportunity for deeper study of the Scriptures as time permits.
- *An open spirit.* Expect the Holy Spirit to speak to you as you read. We believe God will give you ideas for business breakthroughs as you read these memos with your spirit wide open to hear from His Spirit.

It has been a special joy to work together on this book as a father/son team. When Jonathan was a teenager, I (David) shared my heart with him to see new, invigorated economies rise under Christ's control in underserved nations. "If I had a second life to give to world missions," I told him, "I would devote it to rebuilding the decimated infrastructures of poorer nations."

Today, as vice-president of Global Advance, Jonathan has birthed, developed, and now leads Marketplace Missions

Conferences in many of the world's neediest nations. Very encouraging signs from these conferences point to a new day for many of the world's most ravaged economies. Often, Kingdom Business Networks and other initiatives emerge from these life-changing training events.

Many of the principles taught in these conferences are shared in this book. It is our confident hope that *Marketplace Memos* will find its way to the desks (and hearts) of thousands of marketplace missionaries throughout our nation and in many other nations.

Christ calls us to be salt and light in the world.[2] He also calls us to be His ambassadors, representing the interests of His eternal Kingdom wherever we are.[3] Your very presence in the marketplace can become a beachhead for the extension of Christ's Kingdom. We dedicate this book to Christian businesspersons who understand that they are called as Christ's ambassadors — as marketplace missionaries. It is our prayer that your life and influence will yield a maximum return for God's Kingdom purposes in this generation.

— David Shibley and Jonathan Shibley

Part I

TRUE RICHES

Thinking Biblically about Money and Wealth

Giving Living

Years ago, a disgruntled man stormed up to Bob Pierce, founder of World Vision and Samaritan's Purse, after he heard Dr. Pierce preach. The angry man snarled, "I guess all there is to this Christianity is give, give, give." Reflecting later on that encounter Dr. Pierce chuckled, "It just goes to show that even with the wrong spirit a man can get some revelation and truth!"[1]

The often-quoted maxim — "You make a living by what you get, but you make a life by what you give" — is true. Here are seven practical benefits of giving for God's Kingdom purposes and the fulfilling of the Great Commission.

Your gift goes where you may never go. Your gift is an extension of yourself. You receive money in exchange for your investment of time and life. So when you give for Kingdom purposes, in a real sense you're giving a part of yourself. Your gift says you want your life to count for what is eternal. Americans are generous, and Christians in America are especially so. There are many legitimate causes, but I don't know anywhere givers can get more done for the dollar than in giving to world missions.

Giving living loosens the grip of materialism. I noticed a bumper sticker on the back of a sports car that read, "The man who dies with the most toys . . . wins." But Jesus taught that the man who dies with the most "toys" is a short-sighted fool.[2] It's time for us to stop loving cars and clothes and start loving countries! If God so loved the world that He gave His Son, we need to so love the world that we invest in being sure everyone everywhere hears about His Son. I've driven through the poverty-drenched streets of Kolkata and the wealth-lined avenues of Beverly Hills. In both environments I saw desperate people. Jesus wasn't kidding when He warned, *"Beware of covetousness because one's life does not consist in the abundance of things he possesses."*[3] God calls us to embrace biblical prosperity while rejecting materialism. We *can* do both; we *must* do both.

You experience the eternal principle of sowing and reaping. Some churches in Africa practice a unique form of church discipline. If a professing Christian is living in sin, he is allowed to come to church, but he is not allowed to give! When the offering plate comes to him, the usher places his hand over the plate and prevents him from giving. It is a powerful statement that the blessing of God is literally being prevented from coming to the unrepentant man's life. It's an eternal law woven into the very fabric of the universe. Farmers call it the law of sowing and reaping. Scientists refer to it as cause and effect. It's reinforced throughout the Scriptures. The pattern is clear: you must sow in order to reap.

You lay up treasures in heaven. Jesus taught, *"Do not lay up for yourselves treasures on earth . . . but lay up for yourselves treasures in heaven . . . for where your treasure is, there your heart will be also."*[4] A businessman once approached me and said, "I need more of a heart for missions. What should I do?" I replied, "Write out a $2,500 check for missions and sow it to the harvest, and I promise you, you'll have more of a heart for missions."

It just works that way. Where your treasure is (present tense), there your heart will be (future tense). Although "you can't take it with you," you can send it on ahead! This very day you can lay up treasures in heaven.

God calls us to embrace biblical prosperity while rejecting materialism.

God will supply your every need. Are you ready for a jolt? Philippians 4:19 is not a promise for every Christian! It's a great verse: *"My God shall supply all your need according to His riches in glory by Christ Jesus."* But it is not a *carte blanche* to be claimed at will by anybody. No, this promise is given exclusively to those who invest in advancing the gospel.

Read the context. Paul told the Philippians they were the only church that had invested to send him on his first missionary journey. As a result of their gift to launch Paul to the nations, he promised that God would supply their every need. Yes, you can claim Philippians 4:19 *if* you give for the advance of the gospel.

You experience the joy of making a difference in the world. I make no apologies for challenging American Christians to tear loose from some of their money and give it to advance Kingdom causes worldwide. Jesus taught, *"To whom much is given, from him much will be required."*[5] With blessing comes accountability. There is a longing inside every true Christ-follower to make a difference for Him. We do not bear sole responsibility for world evangelization, but because of our affluence and influence, we do bear heightened responsibility.

You experience the significance of participating in God's global purposes. A businessman thanked me for the opportunity to give to Global Advance. He tearfully said, "You give me purpose." For this man, building his company is not the bottom line. He goes beyond the bottom line to build Christ's Kingdom through building his company.

You move past mere success to true significance by aligning your life with God's primary purpose. God's primary purpose is to see His Son known, loved, and worshiped by redeemed people from every tribe and nation. And you are part of that plan. Live to give.

DAY_____DATE_____

DAILY PLANNER

Remember: *"Give and it will be given to you: good measure, pressed down, shaken together, and running over will be put into your bosom. For with the same measure that you use, it will be measured back to you"* (Luke 6:38).

Reflect: "What do your offerings say about your heart levels of gratitude and love for God? What does your spending say about what's truly important on this earth?" — Robert Morris[6]

Pray: That God will make you a joyful giver to His Kingdom causes.

Act: Where is the Holy Spirit directing you to invest for Christ's Kingdom today?

2

Money: Trap or Tool?

Money is one of the greatest tools on earth. It gives options. It gets things accomplished. Money is trapped energy in folded form. It has the power to do enormous good in the lives of others. When rightly managed, it can help a household run smoothly and a business operate well. Money, when used as a tool for blessing, can add dignity, value, and opportunities to people's lives. When misused, money can have devastating effects. The Bible says the love of money is the root cause of all kinds of evil practices.[1] At the heart of the drug industry is money. The root of the porn business is money. Prostitution, gambling, you name it — it's about money.

As Christians, the money God entrusts to us is intended to be used as a tool to glorify Him. But if money is a tool, then why do some have so much more than others?

It's important to understand our primary calling in life. Once we know what lane to drive in, we need to stay in our lane. Not all of us are called to be CEOs or high-level managers. Some are called to lead from the middle of the pack, or even from the lower rung. It really doesn't matter our occupational position as long as God's call on our lives is our primary focus. When we're tuned in to His purposes being accomplished through us, it directly affects our vocation, relationships, and time management.

Our checkbooks are not just a record of our financial transactions; they are a diary of our priorities.

God has already promised to meet our every need.[2] He promises to more than take care of us in the way of food, shelter, clothes, and emotional needs. None of us should want in any of those areas.[3] But He wants to bless us far beyond the basic provisions of life. When looking at things strictly from a financial perspective, it may be that the level of financial blessings in our lives is directly linked to our specific callings. Not everyone needs millions of dollars to accomplish God's will and plans for his life. Some people will need millions and some will require billions to carry out God's assignment for them. We need to mature to the point of understanding that money is simply a tool. It is not a measuring stick of success, significance, or personal worth. There are those who teach that wealth is a sign of God's blessing and therefore (in their minds) a part of godliness. But in fact, Scripture warns us to withdraw from those who equate gain with godliness.[4] Some of the most Christ-honoring, productive people in the Kingdom of God are "poor" by the world's standards.[5] In eternity they will have a great reward. If you have been given much in the realm of finances, accept it with humility, responsibility, stewardship, generosity, and a sobering realization that it all came from God.[6] Also, it can all take wings and fly away.[7] If you find yourself with modest financial provision, you should thank God and seek to be a great steward of what you have. If you find yourself in need of money, you need to go back to the basics and claim the promises of God.

Jesus was specific about where our treasure should be. He taught, *"Do not lay up for yourselves treasures on earth."* Then He told us why — because they have a short shelf life. Concerning earthly treasures, *"moth and rust destroy and . . . thieves break in and steal."* Instead, Jesus said to *"lay up for yourselves treasures in heaven, where neither moth nor rust destroys and where thieves do not break in and steal."*

Then He went on to give this extremely important life principle: *"For where your treasure is, there your heart will be also."*[8] His point is clear: If you need a change of heart, you need to redirect your assets. Put your money where your heart ought to be. You see, our checkbooks are not just a record of our financial transactions;

they are a diary of our priorities. As God gives you clear vision and direction for your life and business, the amount of money necessary for the task will become clearer. If you need more tools for the task, ask for them. God is a giver. And ask for wisdom and guidance to be an honorable steward of what you already have. As we prove ourselves faithful stewards, we will be entrusted with more tools!

DAY_____DATE_____

DAILY PLANNER

Remember: *"For the love of money is a root of all kinds of evil"* (1 Timothy 6:10).

Reflect: "When Jesus is your Master, money serves you, but if money is your master, you become its slave." — Rick Warren[9]

Pray: For God to give you clarity regarding your calling and show you how to better use money as a tool to accomplish His purposes.

Act: Your money is a tool to be used for God's glory. Use this tool today to glorify God, meet human needs, and help fulfill your calling.

3

Money Musings

It should be of more than passing interest to any businessperson that the Bible gives more attention to money than any other subject. The nature of money, how it is acquired, and how it is distributed — these issues matter deeply to God.

Sixteen of Jesus' 38 parables dealt with how to handle money and possessions. One out of every ten verses in the gospels deals with stewarding possessions. Those who count such things estimate that the Bible contains some 500 verses about prayer, some 500 verses about faith, and some 2,000 verses on how we acquire and use money and possessions. Obviously this is a topic that has God's attention — and it ought to have ours.

One of the most important economic questions we can ever grapple with is *how much is enough?* It is our firm conviction that God desires to bless us in every dimension of life, including our finances. After all, you cannot impart what you do not possess. But this begs the serious question — at what point does our focus shift from acquiring to blessing others and the nations? The teaching of Scripture is that we are to embrace prosperity and at the same time, renounce materialism. If your credit cards were all paid off, would that be enough for you? What if there were no debt on your home and cars? What if you had structured your finances to ensure that you and your spouse could live comfortably all your lives — and you were still able to leave an inheritance to your children and grandchildren[1] and give substantially to God's work? Would that then be enough?

Let's review some things the Bible says about this important subject.

God, not His blessings, is the true reward. The greatest blessing in life is not material. Life's greatest treasure is to know God.[2] After God had showered Abraham with enormous wealth, He pulled him aside and reminded him, *"I am your reward."*[3]

Wealth is not necessarily a sign of godliness. There are obvious examples of this everywhere, yet some misguided preachers try to convince us that wealth, in and of itself, is a sign of spirituality and God's favor. Yet the Bible says we are to turn away from those who purport that *"gain is godliness."*[4]

We are not to be overly concerned with material things. They are all perishable. We are to set our affections on what is eternal and live for what will matter forever.[5] John taught that if we are indifferent to the needs of a brother, it is highly questionable if we have God's love within us.[6] John Wesley taught early Methodists to "make all you can, save all you can, give all you can."[7] As medical doctor Richard Swenson observes, "It just seems to me that, according to the investment firm of John (the apostle) and John (Wesley), we should keep our needs low, our generosity high, and our expectations heavenward."[8]

Those who are rich are not to be arrogant or to put their trust in uncertain riches. Riches can quickly take wings and fly away.[9] Our full trust is to be in God alone.[10] If your sense of security is wrapped up in what could potentially be taken from you, you will always battle insecurity.

We are not to be judgmental, either toward those who possess wealth or toward those who do not possess wealth. We should be very careful about putting value judgments on either the poor or the wealthy. We don't have the full story. So, as Pastor Robert Morris admonishes, "Don't fall into the comparison trap. Pride says, 'I earned it.' Poverty says, 'I shouldn't have it.' Gratitude says, 'I received it by grace.' "[11]

We are to learn the lessons both of affluence and need. For most of us, in the span of our lifetime we will probably experience both. In times of affluence, we learn character. In times of need, we learn faith.[12] Paul wrote that he had learned contentment whether in need or whether he had plenty. What was his secret? It was in this context that he wrote, *"I can do all things through Christ who strengthens me."*[13]

Giving should be a way of life for followers of Jesus. God gave His Son.[14] The Son gave His life.[15] The Spirit gives His gifts and His fruit.[16] As lovers of God and partakers of His nature, our lives should also be marked by generosity.[17] This giving spirit begins with tithing our income.[18] God promises to open the windows of heaven and bless those who tithe. Someone has well observed, "God doesn't do windows for less than ten percent." *"God loves a cheerful giver."*[19]

We are to reject all forms of greed. This goes all the way back to the Ten Commandments: *"You shall not covet."*[20] We *are* to love the world (that is, people) and let the beauty of nature point us with gratitude toward God. We *are not* to love the world system or the things of this world.[21] Frivolous spending is denounced throughout Scripture.[22]

Scripture warns against debt.[23] Although debt is woven into the fabric of our society and economy, any debt should be entered into prayerfully, be manageable, and gotten out of as quickly as possible. A lack of debt will free us to greater generosity.[24]

God delights when His servants genuinely prosper.[25] He rewards initiative[26] and honest labor.[27] Biblical prosperity is to live in a healthy relationship with God where all your needs are met, you are giving generously to others, and you are in a position to respond with joy to the promptings of the Holy Spirit to sow into good soil.

Money is to serve us. We are never to serve it. Proper stewardship of money enables us to properly appreciate and receive the true riches.[28] As A.W. Tozer observed, "Any temporal possession can be turned into everlasting wealth. Whatever is given to Christ is immediately touched with immortality."[29]

DAY_____DATE_____

DAILY PLANNER

Remember: *"Through wisdom a house is built, and by understanding it is established; by knowledge the rooms are filled with all precious and pleasant riches"* (Proverbs 24:3–4).

Reflect: "The purpose of prosperity is to give you an opportunity to bring the gospel to the ends of the earth. God will keep adding more and more blessings as you worship Him with the firstfruits of your income. Then you will see the greatest blessing of all — many souls coming into the Kingdom of God!" — Bob Yandian[30]

Pray: That you will honor God in using your money.

Act: As you look at these biblical principles regarding money, allow the Holy Spirit to give you a single, clear directive regarding better stewardship.

4

Possessions

After serving his own jail sentence, Richard Dortch entered another prison to visit his former boss and colleague, Jim Bakker. Richard told me that for several minutes they sat in Bakker's cell and said nothing. They just stared at the blank walls, the bars, the lavatory and toilet. Finally, referring to their lavish days at the now-defunct PTL Television Network, Richard looked at Jim and said, "We really didn't need all that stuff, did we?"

Wealth can be a great blessing from God. But we can't baptize blatant materialism with biblical proof texting. This transgresses the heart of the gospel and the lifestyle of Jesus Himself. God's Word majestically refuses to be the cheerleader of any man-made political or economic system. It stands as the objective judge on all subjects, including economics.

Some people embraced the prosperity message because they saw in it a way to biblically endorse their financial gluttony. Since God is a God of abundance and we are His children, they reasoned that we should have all things in abundance. This message appealed to the inherent greed in people. Yet greed and the tendency to hoard are firmly denounced throughout Scripture.

A wrong conclusion was deduced from a right premise. God *is* a God of abundance. He *does* desire to shower His children with all kinds of blessings. But these blessings are not to stay exclusively ours. As Abraham's spiritual descendants, we are blessed in order to be a blessing to all nations.[1]

23

The Holy Spirit has emphasized prosperity to economically empower the Church to advance Christ's Kingdom. It will take multi-billions of dollars to fulfill the Great Commission. Evangelistic outreaches take money. Missions advances take money. And even in benevolence ministries, somebody has to buy the soup.

God wants to liberate us from debt and from a poverty mentality. He knows that if we are to seize the immense opportunities of this pivotal season, we will need mega-thinkers who are not afraid to invest multi-millions into missions. So He hammers away at the poverty mentality that has historically choked our endeavors. And He raises our faith so we can believe Him for great financial increase.

Scripture is not against having riches — it is against hoarding them.

But instead of using our new-found financial strength to liberate us from financial strain, we sometimes use it as a line of credit for even heavier indebtedness. A drive to keep up appearances of success — whether we're succeeding or not — has infested much of the Church. On this tenuous, deceitful philosophy that success is measured primarily by what we can see or touch, we mortgage our hopes well past our own life span and weigh down our present opportunities with an albatross of debt. We need to remember, as the well-known quote of the late comedian Art Buchwald says, "The best things in life aren't things."

So what constitutes true prosperity or success? To escape the inner city and get a college education is success for the young person who was born there. But it's also success to go back into the thick of the inner city as an agent of transformation. It was success for C.T. Studd to give his fortune to missions and become a faith missionary. It was success for Jim Elliot to say no to a lucrative career in America, become a missionary, and face eventual martyrdom. We cannot view success through the world's distorted lenses. True success is to know God's will for your life and do it with joy.

The question, then, is not whether one has wealth. It is how that wealth is being utilized for God's purposes. Paul said he had learned to live in need and to live in abundance. *"I have learned in whatever situation I am to be content. I know how to be brought low, and I know how to abound. In any and every circumstance, I have learned the secret of facing plenty and hunger, abundance and need."* What was Paul's secret to contentment? *"I can do all things through him [Christ] who strengthens me."*[2] Millions can affirm the truth of Jesus' claim that life does not consist in the abundance of things a person possesses.[3] In Beverly Hills or the crowded, garbage-heaped slums of India, one thing is common: desperate people. Poverty is an insult to the dignity of people. But the pull toward sophisticated idolatry among the rich is equally dehumanizing. As Arthur Gish noted, our society is now so sick that many people "buy things they do not want to impress people they do not like."[4] Martin Luther reminded us, "Our possessions should be in our hands, not in our hearts."[5]

Jesus has set a clear example for us. We are to identify with the weak, the poor, and the dispossessed. We cannot close our ears to the cries of the physically famished in the slums or the spiritually famished in the mansions. It is the same gospel — with the same demands — for a poor leper or a rich, young ruler.

To come to grips with the implications of the gospel is to come to grips with sacrifice. At times in the last several years, I have literally blushed with embarrassment at how some preachers have gleefully promoted teachings almost directly counter to the teachings of Jesus. Some have even inferred that sacrifice is either unspiritual or unscriptural. Whose Bible are they reading?

Scripture is not against *having* riches — it is against *hoarding* them. It is not inordinate to expect a dependable car, a comfortable home, and financial abundance. These accessories often indicate that you are a good steward. It is, however, not only inordinate but also immoral to develop a ravenous lust for "more" because you have somehow bought in to the lie that life does indeed consist in the abundance of things we possess. This is in polar antithesis to the teaching of Jesus. At the end of the day, stuff is just *stuff*.

DAY_____DATE_____

DAILY PLANNER

Remember: *"Watch out! Be on your guard for all kinds of greed; a man's life does not consist in the abundance of his possessions"* (Luke 12:15; NIV).

Reflect: "Let every one of us be guided by that scriptural principle which governed the life of David Livingstone; that we will place no value upon anything we have or may possess, except in its relation to the Kingdom of God." — John R. Mott[6]

Pray: For a biblical understanding of possessions and their true value.

Act: What can you do today to reduce clutter and decrease "stuff" in your life? Are there things you could give away to those in need? Are there things you could sell and give the proceeds to Kingdom causes?

5

Rich Advice

Paul gave some sound counsel to his young pastor protégé, Timothy, as he ended his first letter to him. In fact, it was rich advice — directed specifically to wealthy Christians. Here's the rich advice Paul gave Timothy to pass on to affluent believers.

First, don't be arrogant. And it's not just a suggestion. He said, *"Command those who are rich . . . not to be haughty."* [1] Wealth has the seductive potential to make the affluent think they are intrinsically better than others. And Paul knew how destructive that can be. It's not wealth, but the pride that often latches onto wealth, that sets us up for a downward spiral. *"Pride goes before destruction, and a haughty spirit before a fall."* [2] Arrogance can cloud your judgment so make poor, even fatal, business decisions. But far worse, God Himself resists the proud. Not once, but twice (for added emphasis), the Bible reminds us that God sets Himself in opposition to the proud. [3] No matter how savvy you may be in business, if God opposes you, you're not going very far. The antidote to pride is to proactively humble ourselves daily before God. Have you "made it" financially? Remember, *"It is He who has made us, and not we ourselves."* [4] I know that's talking about God forming us and creating us, but I believe the thought can be broadened. If you've "made it" financially, God enabled you.

Second, don't trust your wealth. Paul is very clear that riches are "uncertain." They are tenuous. You'd better have a pretty healthy equilibrium if you plan to ride today's wild, roller coaster stock market. Notice this warning: *"For riches certainly make themselves wings; they fly away like an eagle toward heaven."*[5] The one thing that is certain about money is that it's not permanent — at least not permanently yours! It takes wings and flies away. No wonder insecurity is pandemic today. If you hang your security on anything that potentially can be taken from you (and that includes money), you will always be insecure. None of this is meant to frighten us or to make us stop investing. But it is meant to sober us to see the limitations of riches.

Third, trust God. While wealth is uncertain, God and His faithfulness are certain. Paul tells Timothy to counsel the wealthy to hang their security on their relationship with God. And Paul reminds us that He is *"the living God."*[6] He is actively at work today — loving you, caring for you, watching over you.

Arrogance can cloud your judgment so you make poor, even fatal, business decisions.

Fourth, enjoy what He has given you. God *"gives us richly all things to enjoy"*[7] and that includes the benefits of wealth. If you can take a vacation, enjoy it! If you have the money to send your kids to college, rejoice! If you're in a position to treat friends to a lovely meal at a great restaurant, have a great time! But remember the source of all these blessings. And also remember God has given us *all things* to enjoy — and that includes the priceless things money can never buy. So enjoy the masterpiece of God's sunset. Enjoy the relationship God has given you with your spouse. Enjoy the freedoms we still have. Enjoy life! And drink deeply of the blessings of your relationship with God and the covenant blessings you have because you know Him.

Having advised wealthy believers how to *think* about money, he now counsels affluent Christians how to *act* in a way that will leverage their wealth for God's Kingdom purposes:

Give. *"Let them do good."*[8] Let them do good by putting their money to work to do what money can do — relieve the poor, build churches, advance the gospel, equip leaders, establish orphanages, train more Kingdom businesspersons . . . and the list goes on. Do good by putting your money to work for Christ and His Kingdom.

Volunteer. Not only is their money to do good, but affluent people themselves are also to be *"rich in good works."*[9] I remember riding through the slums of a city in India with an American millionaire. He looked with compassion on the plight of the people he saw struggling in the squalor outside the car window. Then he turned to me and said, "These trips are important for me. They're a reality check." Throughout that week I saw this affluent businessman roll up his sleeves and be "rich in good works."

Be sensitive to needs and opportunities. Wealthy believers should be *"ready to give"*[10] — poised to seize opportunities — and *"willing to share"*[11] — poised to meet needs.

Live in heaven's honor. Rich Christians are to work today in light of eternity and lay up treasures in heaven, just as Jesus taught.[12] Don't be a Christian existentialist, living only for the present. Live as if heaven matters, because it surely does.

Now, that's rich advice.

DAY_____DATE_____

DAILY PLANNER

Remember: *"Command those who are rich in this present age not to be haughty, nor to trust in uncertain riches but in the living God, who gives us richly all things to enjoy. Let them do good, that they be rich in good works, ready to give, willing to share, storing up for themselves a good foundation for the time to come, that they may lay hold on eternal life"* (1 Timothy 6:17–19).

Reflect: "If a person gets his attitude toward money straight, it will help straighten out almost any other area of his life." — Billy Graham[13]

Pray: For humility, for the ability to leverage wealth in God-honoring ways, for wisdom not to trust in money, and for a glad heart to enjoy all God has given you.

Act: Do good today by giving as God prompts you for Kingdom purposes, invest your time in a worthy volunteer work, be sensitive to Kingdom opportunities and people's needs, and do business today with an eternal perspective.

6

Rich and Empty

I have three friends who fit the profile of the American dream. All are in their thirties and live in spacious houses in prominent, upscale suburbs. Each makes several hundred thousand dollars annually. They have pretty wives and drive sweet rides. Two of the three grew up in Christian homes and attend church regularly. There's just one problem. Beneath the surface they are empty, with plates full of trouble: unstable marriages, anxiety, insecurity. The list goes on.

We see it all the time in our culture. The very things the world says will make us happy end up only disappointing us. It's an elusive dream. Yet people everywhere continue to embrace "the con heard round the world": *If I could just make a hundred grand more. If I could just upgrade the media room. If I could just get that boat. If I just had (fill in the blank)* . . . blah, blah, blah. I go to Third World countries every other month. I witness firsthand the poverty, hardship, and destruction that is part of the daily lives of multiple millions. I see and hear people's pain. Then I come back to the land of plenty and observe the same fallacious, underlying belief: *More money would solve my problems.* It doesn't matter if it's the guy in Africa or the guy in New York City. They both buy into the lie that money will solve their problems and maybe — just maybe — fill the emptiness inside.

If only that were true! Somehow we're wired to believe this. True, money does in fact create options, freedom, and flexibility. These are good things. However, money doesn't bring — cannot bring — lasting peace, joy, or fulfillment. When you cut to the bottom line, these are the things our souls are longing for.

Proverbs 13:7 profiles two men. One man appears rich, yet he is poor. The other man appears poor, but he is rich. When I read this verse, two pictures come to mind. The first is a young man fresh out of college, driving a $50,000 Mercedes on a $45,000 income. The second is a humble, unassuming person who lives modestly yet has millions in the bank. Which of these men would you rather be? True wealth goes far beyond money and material things. True riches are eternal and spring from the heart of God.[1] Who can put a value on skills, character, perspective, peace, purpose, fulfillment, destiny, love, a meaningful existence, and a biblical worldview? Godliness, fleshed out in the marketplace, our communities, churches, and families is invaluable. Passing true wealth on to the next generation is the greatest inheritance you could ever pass down.

When we begin to think biblically concerning what constitutes true wealth, priorities become much clearer. Jesus set the record straight when He told us to seek first His Kingdom and then everything else would fall into place.[2] I believe God wants to lavishly bless His people. Regrettably, however, He has already abundantly blessed so many of us — but what have we done with His blessings? It is tragic when the very blessings God gives us distract us and move us onto a carnal path. Each of us has an appointed time at the Judgment Seat of Christ. That's when it will all shake down. How are we going to answer the Lord regarding what we did with what He gave us? How did our lives contribute to the fulfilling of His assignment (the Great Commission) while we were on the earth? If you stay up at night grappling with issues, these are the real questions that should keep you up at night.

God is looking for a certain type of person who will put His agenda above personal agendas. His eyes are scanning the earth for that type of person, because when He finds him, He's going to strongly back him.[3] Imagine what it really looks like when Almighty God *strongly supports* a business! Scripture is abundantly clear that God will radically bless men and women whose hearts and wallets are fully His. He's looking for those who will produce with what they have rather than waste it all away. The world is waiting for new models. The world needs to see Kingdom-minded businesspersons who understand that the purpose behind their prosperity goes far beyond themselves. Are you a part of that Kingdom?

DAY_____ DATE_____

DAILY PLANNER

Remember: *"There is one who makes himself rich, yet has nothing; and one who makes himself poor, yet has great riches"* (Proverbs 13:7).

Reflect: "Wealth is made up of the ability and character skills that we gain to manage the material world. Riches, in contrast, are primarily material goods that one can gain with or without obedience to God. . . . Wealth may produce riches, but riches cannot produce wealth because wealth comes from obedience to the covenant." — Dennis Peacocke[4]

Pray: For God to help you accumulate true, lasting wealth.

Act: Live each day in preparation to stand before the Lord.

1
The Covenant Cycle

*T*he Bible is not against *having* riches. The Bible is against *hoarding* riches. Riches, wealth, and the blessings of God are never meant to be exclusively ours; they are always to be extended to a world in need.

You and I are in a covenant relationship with God. He has become our God, and we are His children through faith in Jesus Christ.[1] When we enter into this covenant with the one true God, we also become spiritual children of Abraham and heirs of the promises that were made to him.[2] The promise God made to him was in the form of a covenant, a sworn oath God made with him. In this covenant, God promised that Abraham and his children (both natural and spiritual) would be *blessed*, they would *be a blessing*, and that this blessing would extend to *all the families of the earth*.[3] This set in motion what I call "the covenant cycle." It is the way of life for people of faith who truly know God. Because we know Him, we are *blessed*, we are blessed in order that we may *be a blessing*, and we are intentionally to extend that blessing *to all the families (nations and peoples) of the earth*.

This theme — and this pattern — continues throughout Scripture. For the person who truly understands his or her covenant relationship with God, it's as natural as breathing. It becomes the spiritual rhythm of our lives; we are *blessed to be a blessing to everyone, everywhere*. This also explains why, when a believer in Christ fails to live and operate within this covenant cycle, not only does he feel like something is missing, but he can also feel spiritually like he's wanting for air. And in a real sense, he is. He has choked off the flow of God's covenant life to him and through him.

Many preachers enjoy quoting the verse that reminds us, *". . . it is [God] who gives you the ability to produce wealth."* But too often they don't quote the rest of the verse that tells us *why* we are given this ability: *"and so confirms his covenant, which he swore to your forefathers."*[4] Do you see it? The covenant cycle is in play once again. We are blessed with the ability to generate wealth so we may "confirm the covenant." In other words, we are *blessed in order to be a blessing to everyone, everywhere.* If God simply gave us the ability to get wealth with no greater purpose than increasing our own wealth, Christianity would indeed be a self-serving and thus weak faith. But God never intends for blessings to be permanently parked with us. We are to extend the blessing beyond us to our city, our nation, and our world.

David picks up the covenant cycle theme in his kingly prayer on behalf of a nation called to be in covenant with God. David prays, *"God be merciful to us and bless us, and cause His face to shine upon us."*[5] David understands that, since they are in covenant with the one true God, they have every right to ask Him, based on His covenant promise, to bless them. But David also knows why they are to be blessed — *"That Your way may be known on earth, Your salvation among all nations."*[6] David gets it. He knows that covenant people are *blessed in order to be a blessing to everyone, everywhere.*

A New Covenant comes to us in Jesus Christ. But in a real sense this New Covenant is a continuum of the promise God has always made to those who are rightly related to Him. Paul picks up on this covenant cycle when he writes, *"Christ has redeemed us . . . that the blessing of Abraham might come upon the Gentiles [all the peoples of the earth] in Christ Jesus, that we might receive the promise of the Spirit through faith."*[7] Christ has redeemed us; that is, He has saved us and blessed us. Because we are saved, we are now the spiritual seed of Abraham and heirs to the blessings given to him and his descendents.[8] We are to extend these blessings by bringing others into a covenant relationship with God. How? By bringing the gospel to them, so that they too might know Christ and receive "the blessings of Abraham." We have been redeemed in order *"that the blessing of Abraham might come upon the [nations] in Christ."*

If any of these three components that make up the covenant cycle are removed, the result is a warped theology. Remove teaching on being blessed and the Church is weakened by a poverty mentality. Remove the call to be a blessing and our faith seems self-centered and self-serving. (By the way, this is why many people — both believers and unbelievers — find the teaching of some TV preachers so repugnant.) Remove the extending of the blessing to all the families of the earth and the Church is crippled by a lack of evangelistic and missionary vision.

Of course, the blessings we have are not merely financial. God has *"blessed us with every spiritual blessing . . . in Christ."*[9] Therefore, the greatest blessing we can bring to the nations is the gospel. *The gospel lifts everything.* The biblical concept of prosperity goes far beyond finances; true wholeness is a life that is full, the kind of life Jesus gives.[10] Covenant people who don't live in the covenant cycle feel as though they are choking spiritually — and they are. God has called you for higher things. He has called you to bless nations! He has commissioned you to disciple and transform nations.[11] He has charged you to *"rebuild the ancient ruins, raise up the age-old foundations,"* be a *"repairer of broken walls"* and a *"restorer of streets with dwellings."*[12]

You have been blessed to be a blessing to all the peoples of the earth.

DAY_____DATE_____

DAILY PLANNER

Remember: *"God be merciful to us and bless us, and cause His face to shine upon us, that Your way may be known on earth, Your salvation among all nations"* (Psalm 67:1–2).

Reflect: "There is too much of a tendency to have a poverty mentality in today's church. Our outlook is too small, but that smallness can be shaken off in answer to our Lord Jesus, who has called us to be *big* people. Big in our worldview. Big in our love for the lost. Big in our giving." — Jack Hayford[13]

Pray: That you will live and operate in the covenant cycle.

Act: Rehearse the blessings you have through faith in Christ. Act today to extend that blessing by sharing your faith with someone who needs Christ. Intentionally extend the blessings cross-culturally through your gifts and abilities.

8

The Money Test

G od allows us to be tested with various things throughout life to refine and develop our character. One of the greatest tests is how we handle money, whether we have little or much. Last year I met a gentleman named Bob. He's a very gentle, kind-hearted man with a well-trimmed beard as white as Santa Claus. I sat in sheer amazement as he told me his story. Bob is dying, and he knows it. At best he has about two years left unless God miraculously heals him. Due to a large settlement, Bob recently got a windfall of money.

Now here's a predicament: Let's say you get 30 million dollars with one catch — you're going to die within the next 24 months. How would you respond? How would I respond? I know a lot of people would be creatively finding ways to spend as much of it as extravagantly and fast as possible. But not Bob. Bob is on his face every day asking God how he can most strategically give it all away. He wants this money to have the biggest possible impact for Kingdom purposes. Bob wants to ace his test.

As I sat and listened to Bob's story, I couldn't help but have this thought: *When you know your appointed day is coming, you begin to get your house in order.* Bob is living every day in light of *that day* when he will be face to face with Jesus. He knows he'll give an account for what he did with what was placed in his hands.

You also have a scheduled, personal appointment with Jesus. The Bible calls it the Judgment Seat of Christ.[1] The apostle Paul warned that our options on that awesome day are either eternal rewards or literally seeing what we have done go up in smoke. *"If any man builds on this foundation using gold, silver, costly stones, wood, hay or straw, his work will be shown for what it is, because the Day will bring it to light. It will be revealed with fire, and the fire will test the quality of each man's work. If what he has built survives, he will receive his reward. If it is burned up, he will suffer loss; he himself will be saved, but only as one escaping through the flames."*[2]

All of us are like Bob. While we may not have a great deal of money at our disposal, like Bob, we each have an appointed time with God. What kind of return on His investment are we going to bring Him from our lives on the earth? What types of materials are we using to construct our lives? Wood? Hay? Straw? Or are we living under the lordship of Christ and the control of the Holy Spirit — building with precious stones, gold, and silver?

Veteran missionary Wayne Myers observed, "When a person is blessed financially, God either gets a jewel or the devil gets a fool."[3] Are you passing your money test? How do you view the money you make? Is it yours or His? Are you a wise steward? Does God have permission to redirect your assets?

One of the most powerful attributes of generosity is its contagious nature. My job allows me to speak to business leaders in many underserved nations. One of the most touching things I've witnessed is their unyielding generosity. Most of the people I speak to have not yet "made it" financially. They have business ideas and small to modest amounts of money. But they also possess an insatiable desire to see God use their businesses for good, not greed. My heart was so touched when a group of 200 business leaders in the Dominican Republic gave over $2,000 toward an upcoming Christian business conference in India. I went to India and told the Christian businesspersons in India about the generosity shown them by their brothers and sisters in Christ in the Dominican Republic. Then the Indian believers got in the game and gave a substantial offering toward training Christian entrepreneurs in Kenya. What a great picture of contagious cross-cultural generosity!

This is God's heart. God wants us to be blessed in order to be a blessing to the nations.[4]

DAY_____DATE_____

DAILY PLANNER

Remember: *"A generous man will himself be blessed"* (Proverbs 22:9; NIV).

Reflect: "I was born selfish but I was born again generous." — Robert Morris[5]

Pray: For God to show you how to build your life on things that will last eternally. Ask Him to show you how to use your resources.

Act: Invest money and energy today in ways that will bring an eternal return.

9
Why Do the ungodly Prosper?

*I*t's a question that irks all of the "good guys."[1] *Why do the ungodly prosper? How come the guy who lies, cheats, and steals is getting all the deals? Why is it that the person who could not care less about using his money for noble causes seems to always strike it rich?* It's one of the main rubs of Christian businesspersons all over the world. When we set our hearts to pursue God in the arena of business, we're bound to get frustrated from time to time at the things we see happening around us. In the midst of these emotional challenges there are several truths we need to remember.

First, God is ultimately in control. Because God is good, *"He makes His sun rise on the evil and on the good, and sends rain on the just and on the unjust."*[2] For a season, even long seasons, the ungodly may indeed prosper financially. Sin's entry into the world injected suffering, inefficiencies, and imperfections.[3] Let's face it. Our world is full of unfairness, injustices, inequality, and questions that make us scratch our heads and wonder why God would allow such a thing. But He *is* in control and because He is holy, righteous, and just, there *will* be a day when justice is served.[4]

Second, we need to step back and look at the larger picture. There will be times in our lives and business when we'll have to make a decision. Will we honor God in this transaction, or will we settle for a short-term gain? Any time an unrighteous act is done, whether in business or any other arena, the gain is short-term. There is pleasure in sin, but that pleasure has a short shelf life.[5]

Every day you're sowing seeds toward your future and future generations. You may have to lose out on a deal or get the short end of the stick because you chose righteousness. But when you plant righteous seeds through your actions, they will produce a harvest in due time.[6] Blessings and reward will come to you. God guarantees it. It always pays to be *"doing the will of God from the heart, with goodwill doing service, as to the Lord, and not to men, knowing that whatever good anyone does, he will receive the same from the Lord."*[7]

Third, there may be more at play under the surface. Godly principles work, no matter who is putting them into practice. It could be that a greedy, selfish person is applying biblical principles at work without even realizing it. Thus, his business prospers, even though the person may be a jerk to work with. For instance, an ardent atheist who pays his bills on time will be better thought of in the business arena than a vocal Christian who is consistently late in paying invoices. On the flip side, God is concerned about refining our character. In a sense, earth is eternity's workshop. God sometimes allows difficult circumstances to refine our character and prepare us for greater things to come.

The Bible advises us not to be upset when the ungodly prosper. *"Do not fret because of evildoers, nor be envious of the workers of iniquity. For they shall soon be cut down like the grass."*[8] Defying God and His ways eventually catches up with a person. Note this serious warning: *"When the wicked spring up like the grass, and when all the workers of iniquity flourish, it is that they may be destroyed forever."*[9] How's that for a destiny? The wicked are compared to a blade of grass or a weed that quickly pops up but then withers away.

The promise of the righteous is that we will inherit the land. The rewards God has for those who endure in righteousness are almost too amazing to comprehend.[10] In Matthew 19:29, Jesus encourages those who have paid a personal price in losing something of value to follow Him. He promises those who count the cost to follow Him will receive 100 times as much as was lost *and* eternal life. What a deal! In the context of this passage, He's referring to those who have lost community or family relationships. He promises to more than make up for what was lost.

Suppose you were having a tight month and someone you trust came to you and said, "If you give me a thousand dollars today, in a week I'll give you $100,000." Would you do it? It might be that you temporarily miss the $1,000 and have to make a sacrifice to give it, but it would be well worth the cost for the future reward. Let's not misunderstand. Jesus isn't promoting a get-rich-quick scheme. He is offering us an even better deal. Jesus is offering us *a life* that is a hundred times richer than the life of one who is obsessed with money. He promises not only a one hundred-fold return on what is lost or given up, but also a priceless and incomparable bonus of abundant and eternal life!

So, back to the ungodly. What you see is what they get. They have their reward. It is short term and will soon be gone. Don't become discouraged when it seems like the bad guys are winning. Remember that those who are followers of Christ will be the real and lasting winners — in this life and the next.

DAY_____ DATE_____

DAILY PLANNER

Remember: *"Do not fret because of evildoers, nor be envious of the workers of iniquity, for they shall soon be cut down like the grass, and wither as the green herb. Trust in the Lord, and do good; dwell in the land and feed on His faithfulness"* (Psalm 37:1–2).

Reflect: Look up these further verses regarding rewards for the righteous: 1 Corinthians 9:25; 1 Thessalonians 2:19–20; James 1:12.

Pray: Make a conscious decision to honor God no matter the outcome.

Act: Rehearse the blessings you have through faith in Christ. Act today to extend that blessing by sharing your faith with someone who needs Christ. Intentionally extend the blessings cross-culturally through your gifts and abilities.

Part II

KINGDOM BUSINESS

Your Marketplace Ministry

10

Big Business

One of the people who had a primary influence on my life as a young preacher was John Frank, an artist and business entrepreneur. John Frank was a creative sculptor, a potter. His Frankoma Pottery is sought after by collectors worldwide. He was the first businessman to believe in me as a teenage preacher to the point of investing financially. I'll never forget sitting in his office when I was 19. There was fire in my eyes as a young evangelist, and there was a sparkle in his eyes as he joyfully gave to advance the gospel. He modeled a joyful giver. I believe he had the spiritual gift of giving.[1] I even watched him laugh with glee more than once as he wrote out generous checks to further God's work.

That day in his office, while writing a check that literally got me down the road for the next evangelistic outreach, Mr. Frank looked at me with obvious delight and exclaimed, "This soul-winning is big business!"

Indeed, it is. And that's why living witnesses are so well suited for the marketplace. The pulpit was a later invention of the Church and organized evangelistic meetings were invented only in the last 200 years. But the initial spread of the good news was trafficked through commerce, in public discourses, and through relationships of friends and business associates. Ed Sivoso reminds us that almost all of Jesus' miracles happened in the marketplace.[2] Only a few were in officially designated houses of worship. Christ's light and life are meant for public display — for the street, where we eat, and where we meet.

Is soul-winning "big business" in your mind and heart? It can be. Your office can be — and should be — a beachhead for the spread of the Kingdom of God. You can impact your world for Jesus Christ. Here are three practical ways.

You can *live* the gospel. *Witness* is a noun more than a verb. In other words, witnessing is first of all something we *are*, and secondarily it is something we *do*. Jesus said His followers are light in a dark world.[3] Because the light of Christ is in us, we are to intentionally position ourselves so that His light might have maximum impact.[4] And we are to live in such a way that our good deeds will cause people to glorify God.[5]

Too often Christians in America are perceived as mean-spirited and constantly adversarial. Yet the Bible teaches that we are to engage our culture with a winsomeness that always has fruitful evangelism as its goal. Paul said he found common ground with diverse sectors of society for a single purpose: *"that I might win"* people to Christ. Why did he act with grace and courtesy toward everyone? *"For the gospel's sake."*[6]

You can *give* the gospel. Paul commended the Philippian church for its partnership with him financially to make possible his first missionary journey. It was in the context of expressing his appreciation that he also gave the promise, *"My God will supply all your need according to His riches in glory by Christ Jesus."*[7] In other words, it was because they had invested in what is dear to God's heart — the advance of the gospel — that He guaranteed their needs would be met.

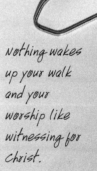

Nothing wakes up your walk and your worship like witnessing for Christ.

When the Iron Curtain fell, an American soft drink company invested close to a billion dollars to open the new eastern European market. Coca-Cola invested strategically and massively for the purpose of getting their product on the lips of millions of new customers. How much are we willing to risk to see the name of Jesus on the lips of millions of new believers?

Pastor Robert Morris notes, "Use your money to affect people — to help them hear the gospel — and they will form part of your welcoming committee when you get to heaven."[8] What a great thought — and what a motivation to invest financially to spread the gospel!

You can *tell* the gospel. Nothing wakes up your walk and worship like opening your mouth and witnessing for Jesus Christ. Paul urged a wealthy businessman to *"be active in sharing your faith, so that you will have a full understanding of every good thing we have in Christ."*[9] You have a circle of influence that is absolutely unique to you. Just look for opportunities to share your faith in Christ. In fact, the latest two places I've led someone to Christ were a gas station and a restaurant.

The most common biblical analogies for evangelism — fishing and farming — are intentional, deliberate acts. They are both vocations. So it should just be natural *in our business* to share the gospel. Jesus said that a sure sign that we are following Him is that we become *"fishers of men."*[10] It follows, then, that if we're not fishing, we're not following. Evangelism is always a part of true discipleship. And there is no better place to share our faith than the marketplace.

There is really no difference between work and ministry. In fact, they come from the same root word in the original Greek language. While pastors may have 2 or 3 hours each week to influence people, marketplace ministers have at least 40 hours. So let your light shine.[11] If you will reflect Christ's character, ultimately many of your fellow-workers will find Him. That's why marketplace ministry is a major key to revival.

As you are sensitive to the Holy Spirit, He will prompt you to boldly yet tactfully share your faith in Christ. Don't ever be ashamed of the gospel.[12] And as you live a God-honoring life of integrity, spiritually hungry co-workers will often ask you about your faith. Be prepared. *"Always be prepared to give an answer to everyone who asks you the reason for the hope that you have. But do this with gentleness and respect."*[13]

By sovereign grace it has fallen on our generation to have within our grasp that for which other generations of Christians have prayed, dreamed, and died — closure on the Great Commission. And if it is not this generation of Christians — we who have seen God's gracious renewal, we who possess more data on global harvest than any previous generation, we who stand on the shoulders of 20 centuries of missionary giants — if it is not us God wants to use to evangelize the world, then who else is it?

DAY_____DATE_____

DAILY PLANNER

Remember: *"The fruit of the righteous is a tree of life, and he who wins souls is wise"* (Proverbs 11:30).

Reflect: "I am not here merely to enjoy the good life. I am here as a child and a servant of God to invest my time, my talent, and my treasure to seek and to save the lost. This is what our Lord came to do 2,000 years ago, and what He commanded His followers to do generation after generation until His blessed return." — Bill Bright[14]

Pray: Ask the Holy Spirit for boldness to share your faith in Christ, and for sensitivity to His prompting to witness for Christ.

Act: Look for specific ways today that you can live for the gospel, give for the gospel, and speak for the gospel.

11

Business by Revelation

fter a futile night of catching nothing, Jesus challenged the self-sure Peter to *"launch out into the deep and let down your nets for a catch."*[1] He was prodding him to go against conventional wisdom and standard business procedures — just as He may be prodding you to do today.

What is Jesus calling you to do today that may be unusual? Will you obey Him? When Jesus speaks to you regarding a business problem or opportunity, *always listen* and *always obey*. Yes, God is the author of reason. He has given humans reasoning capacities, and that is the standard way we are to operate and assess business challenges — unless He speaks otherwise. Our *modus operandi* should be to think . . . but then hear and obey. Think — use the reasoning capacities God has given you. But also hear — expect to hear in your spirit a clear directive as to how to proceed. And sometimes, what you hear will be a call to the unconventional.

Are you listening for His voice? Not only has God *spoken* through His book[2] and through His Son,[3] God *is still speaking*. The Bible is our ultimate authority. But God did not become mute nor did His people become deaf the day the canon of Scripture was closed. Jesus said that we are to live by this *rhema* of His revelation and directives.[4] We must attune our spirits to His Spirit.[5] And His declarations are usually not dramatic; the King of the universe often speaks in *"a still, small voice."*[6]

God will never tell you to violate what He has already clearly laid down in His Word. Nor will He nullify reason — but He may supersede it. God never defies what He creates; but He is Lord over all He creates. What may appear to us as *irrational* is not — not if Jesus has spoken it. God is not irrational, but He sometimes operates in a suprarational way; that is, He supersedes what we think is the reasonable thing to do.

And when He speaks, be careful not to "back talk" to Jesus. When Peter retorted, *"Master, we have toiled all night and caught nothing,"*[7] it may have been his veiled way of saying, "We're the fishermen around here, Lord. It's our profession. We know a 'dry hole' when we see one. We've studied this. We've got a lot of experience and expertise in this area. You just be Master of the 'religious stuff' and we'll take care of business."

Trust me — you are *not* smarter than Jesus, not even when it comes to business. Peter may have been the man who knew how to fish, but Jesus was the Man who *made* the fish. His "know how" will always trump yours.

Thank God, Peter didn't end his response to Jesus there. *"Nevertheless,"* he continued, *"at Your word I will let down the net."*[8] For someone reading this today, it's time to stop whining to Jesus about your meager results although you've been doing all you know to do. It's time to stop fishing in shallow water, and time to start obeying His unconventional directive to you, and start expecting a miracle.

Notice Jesus' two directives to Peter: *"Launch out into the deep."* In other words, "Go beyond your depth. Go into the uncharted waters. Just trust Me, and trust My word to you." For whatever reason, is there still some residual reticence in you that fears going into the unknown? Are you afraid you might actually *succeed*? Bring your fears to Jesus. Let Him take you into new territory, new waters.

"Let down your nets for a catch." Now your training can go to work. Jesus didn't tell Peter, "I'll do it for you." Instead, He told Peter to do what *he* could do, to set the stage for Him to do what only *He* could do.

Put the systems in place to retain the blessing God is about to bring to you. And expect a miracle. Even if, like Peter, you have worked all night with sparse results, when Jesus speaks — get moving, and get ready!

Peter was only prepared for what had always been. He had a sufficient number of nets of sufficient dimensions to accommodate the size of the "catch" to which he was accustomed. But Jesus wants to give you *more* — much more. If you will obey His word to you, He will bring you a back-breaking, boat-sinking load! He wants your "catch" to be huge, so that the glory that goes to Him will be huge.[9] If you let Jesus start calling the shots in your business, are your present "nets" big enough to accommodate what would happen?

Interestingly, a similar incident happened over three years later. Again, Jesus told experienced businessmen — fishermen — to fish in an unconventional way. And again, the results were nothing short of miraculous.[10]

So think. Use the reasoning powers God has given you. But don't stop there. Hear. Then, obey. Jesus said that a telltale sign of those who truly know Him is that they hear His voice, and they obey what they hear. He said, *"My sheep hear my voice . . . and they follow Me."*[11]

He's speaking now — to you. No matter how dismal your past attempts, *go deeper. Get bigger.*

DAY_____DATE_____

DAILY PLANNER

Remember: *"Launch out into the deep and let down your nets for a catch"* (Luke 5:4).

Reflect: "Disturb us, Lord, when we are too well pleased with ourselves, when our dreams have come true because we have dreamed too little, when we have arrived safely because we sailed too close to the shore. . . . Disturb us, Lord, to dare more boldly, to venture on wider seas where storms will show Your mastery, where losing sight of land we shall find the stars. We ask You to push back the horizons of our hopes; and to push into the future with strength, courage, hope, and love." — Sir Francis Drake[12]

Pray: For grace to hear clearly the voice of the Lord, and courage to act on what you hear.

Act: Think. Hear. Obey.

12

Favor

*N*othing could be more vital than finding favor with God. God is scanning the earth today, looking for those He can lift to highly favored status and use as His instruments to fulfill His purposes in this generation.

All believers in Christ live under the general grace of God, but there are certain individuals who seem to be "highly favored" by Him. How can you become highly favored by God?

God is constantly scanning the earth, looking for a certain quality of person, one *"whose heart is loyal to Him."* When He finds that kind of sold-out loyalty, He will *"show Himself strong on behalf"* of that person.[1]

Mary, the mother of Jesus, *"found favor with God."*[2] In fact, the angel Gabriel referred to her as *"highly favored."*[3] What did God see in Mary that so impressed Him? If we can discover the qualities of heart Mary possessed that brought her to God's attention and made her "highly favored," we can cultivate those same qualities in our lives — and be used by God, as she was, to bring forth the light of Jesus in our day. It needs to be clearly understood that we are not worshiping Mary, something she herself would have opposed. Mary acknowledged her own need of a Savior when she said, *"My spirit has rejoiced in God my Savior."*[4] But her life is an awesome example of how to find God's favor. So what were the qualities of heart Mary possessed that brought her favor with God?

Mary had **a pure heart.** She was *"a virgin . . . engaged to be married."*[5] She was pledged to a good man named Joseph. And though Mary loved Joseph, she loved God more. She determined to keep herself pure before God and thus be a vessel of honor. Whatever your past may be, from this day forward you can live with a pure heart and receive God's favor. *"'Come now, and let us reason together,' says the Lord, 'though your sins are like scarlet, they shall be white as snow; though they are red like crimson, they shall be as wool.'"*[6]

Mary also had **a daring heart.** She was willing to risk greatly for God. When the angel's annunciation came to Mary, she knew well the possible consequences. Yet without hesitation she responded, *"Behold, the maidservant of the Lord! Let it be to me according to your word."*[7] Her deepest, core identity was not as Joseph's fiancée, but as the servant of the Lord. She knew that saying yes to God meant risking her engagement and reputation. Yet Mary was willing to give God what was most precious to her. Are you willing to give God what is most precious to you?

This handmaid of the Lord also had **a faith-filled heart.** Faith was so obvious in Mary's life that when Elizabeth greeted her she blessed her for her faith: *"Blessed is she who believed, for there will be a fulfillment of those things which were told her from the Lord."*[8] Not only did Mary have great faith, she had faith to believe for something that had never happened in history. Never had there been a virgin birth, but Mary said yes and believed. Today God is looking for men and women who will believe for what has never yet happened. Today, will you say yes to God and believe?

Then, Mary possessed **a worshiping heart.** Her response to God's miracle in her life was to fill her heart and her mouth with worship. *"My soul magnifies the Lord,"* she exclaimed, *"and my spirit has rejoiced in God my Savior."*[9] Her great *Magnificat*[10] is a beautiful hymn of praise and worship to God. The Holy Spirit is calling out marketplace worshipers who will bring His presence into the corridors of power.

Mary's song of worship was full of Scripture. She had **a Word-filled heart.** She personalized Scripture and wove it back into a

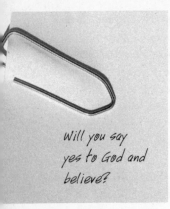

Will you say yes to God and believe?

glorious paean of worship. Like Mary, we should hide God's Word in our heart and release it back to Him in worship.

Mary also guarded a **hope-filled heart.** She was willing to forego honor in her own generation in order to build a spiritual path for generations to come. Although maligned in her own lifetime, every succeeding generation has honored her. She looked to the future and knew that all future generations *"will call me blessed."*[11] Today, as well, God is looking for those who will lay aside their reputation in radical obedience to Jesus Christ and build a spiritual heritage for those who follow.

Now, let's fast-forward 30 years. Jesus is beginning His ministry at the marriage of Cana. When they ran out of wine, Mary preached the greatest sermon ever: *"Whatever He says to you, do it."*[12] Above all, Mary had **a surrendered heart.** Having made a full surrender decades earlier, she instantly chose obedience to God's purposes rather than her own plans. And she found favor with God. You can, too.

DAY_____DATE_____

DAILY PLANNER

Remember: *"I entreated Your favor with my whole heart"* (Psalm 119:58).

Reflect: "Whenever you see a successful business, someone once made a courageous decision." — Peter Drucker[13]

Pray: For God's favor on your life (1 Chronicles 4:10).

Act: What qualities of heart that Mary possessed do you need to work on?

13

Focus and Follow Through

*I*f you are going to accomplish anything significant, it will require focus, follow-through, and unflinching determination. The ability of any leader to focus always reverts back to vision. What is the vision for your life, your family, your ministry, and your company? The ability to maintain clarity of vision becomes more difficult as time goes on. Unforeseen pressures mount and unpredictability occurs.

We can stay focused on what's really important if we live by priorities, not preferences. I love what Rick Warren says: "If you don't live by priorities, you'll live by pressure. There is no other option. Either you determine what's important in life or other people will determine it for you."[1] So true!

It seems clear that God works His wonders — and runs the universe — according to set patterns. Universal principles such as sowing and reaping and seedtime and harvest are applicable to many facets of life. In Jesus' parable of the seeds, only one out of four seeds produced fruit, but the seed that *did* produce was extremely fruitful. This is a relatively universal principle that can be applied to marketing, sales, and forecasting.

In management theory, the "Pareto principle" or the "80/20 principle" has been heralded widely. This principle's premise is that 20 percent of the people create 80 percent of the overall productivity. Also, 20 percent of the people generate 80 percent of the profits. Pareto's principle can also be applied to our focus of effort. We should pour our energy and time into the 20 percent of activities that will make an 80 percent difference in overall operations.

Great leaders are able to identify these patterns. They focus on their strengths and pour their energy into the things that will produce the most fruit. Think of the clarity of focus in Ronald Reagan's presidency. Even his opponents could easily identify his focus: Defeat communism and cut taxes. Focus must be applied to your calling, your motivations, your family, and your work. Each of these arenas of life should complement the others.

The world does not lack for good ideas; it lacks for the implementing of good ideas.

If you could do just three things in the next year that would make a significant impact in your life or business, what would those three things be? What about in the next three months? How about today? If you can answer those questions within each time frame, you will be on your way to a focused, productive life.

With Paul, we should be able to say, *"This one thing I do."*[2] Jim Collins picked up on this in his book, *Good to Great*. He suggests that a leader who identifies one unifying "hedgehog principle" and bases his decisions on that is more likely to achieve "greatness" than a leader who is pulled in many different directions.[3] For Christians in the marketplace, our "hedgehog principle" is an integrated, biblical worldview that motivates us to do everything for God's glory and the extension of His Kingdom.

Not only do great leaders learn to focus, they commit to following through on their focused priorities. Follow-through requires ruthless determination. There are so many distractions that war against our focus. Often *good* things can crowd out the truly *great* things. If we're focused and have a plan, we will be able to more easily decipher between the two.

Follow-through and determination go hand in hand. We can all probably remember a point in our lives when a great plan was never implemented. We just didn't follow through. Jesus spoke clearly to the need for follow-through: *"For which of you, intending to build a tower, does not sit down first and count the cost, whether he has enough to finish it — lest, after he has laid the foundation, and is not able to finish, all who see it begin to mock him, saying, 'This man began to build and was not able to finish.'"*[4]

Nobody respects a job half-completed. Jesus is saying to carefully plan our actions and follow through. It will take focus and determination to be a *finisher*. The world does not lack for good ideas; it lacks for the *implementing* of good ideas. No matter how spectacular the dream, at some point dreams must be translated into the real world of work. Our generation needs examples of godly finishers who are able to focus on things that matter and finish the job.

If you lack focus and direction then go back to the big picture — the vision God has put in your heart. Allow that vision to become clear again in your mind and heart. Then, determine to finish the big thing God put you on earth to do.[5]

DAY_____DATE_____

DAILY PLANNER

Remember: *"For which of you, intending to build a tower, does not sit down first and count the cost, whether he has enough to finish it — lest, after he has laid the foundation, and is not able to finish, all who see it begin to mock him, saying, 'This man began to build and was not able to finish' "* (Luke 14:28–30).

Reflect: "While broad exposure and wide-ranging interests are important, leaders who offer the most lasting contributions incorporate their exposure into a laser focus." — Harold Myra and Marshall Shelly[6]

Pray: That you will be a focused finisher.

Act: Apply Pareto's 80/20 principle to your business. What three things could you do that would make a significant impact in your life over the next year? The next three months? Today?

14

Globalization

We hear a lot in the news about globalization and its effect on international economies. Many people have mixed feelings on the subject. Some feel it hurts our nation's economy because we can't compete with lower labor costs in other nations. But have you ever stopped to think that God might be strategically orchestrating all of this? Could it be that this is a divine setup to unleash God's people into making a relevant impact worldwide?

Twenty years ago most people couldn't imagine that China would be a major economic player in the world. India used to be considered the epitome of a Third World country in many people's minds. Yet today India boasts one of the world's fastest-growing economies. Other nations like Brazil and South Africa are showing promising economic development. There are countless economic opportunities in underdeveloped nations.

What does this say about the world we live in today? I believe God is prodding believers, especially Christians in the marketplace, to wake up and see the harvest around us! Commerce is opening new doors for the gospel that traditional missionary efforts were never able to open! Many nations that would typically be closed to overt Christian missions efforts are very open to economic development. This bodes well for savvy, Great Commission-minded businesspersons who want to be used by God in the global arena of commerce.

Back in the 1800s in the interior of Africa, the great missionary David Livingstone wrote in his journals that Christian merchants combined with missionaries could eradicate slavery. Livingstone saw the enormous impact Christianity and commerce could have on a continent. I believe he was seeing with spiritual eyes the heart God has for the nations. We are called to display a holistic Christianity lived out in such a way that it touches major sectors of society and culture.

Today is no different. God is giving many men and women visions of forming "Great Commission companies" that will be used to glorify God throughout the nations. These businesses will generate resources that will bless multitudes and point them to a new life in Jesus Christ. Many of these businesses are being formed in underdeveloped nations to bless communities and nations both spiritually and economically. Employees who are hired are exposed either directly or indirectly to God's love and His characteristics through a God-glorifying work culture that is created and nurtured. Others see their businesses as a funding mechanism to bless various Kingdom initiatives. Some businesses are finding favor with government leaders and opportunities to influence "gatekeepers" for Christ. There is an elevated level of purpose and energy that comes to a businessperson when he sees his business as ministry. God wants to use His people in the marketplaces of the world to bring spiritual hope to the lost and tangible solutions to problems that plague societies, communities, and nations. There is no place like the marketplace to show off the glory and splendor of Almighty God!

Think of the eternal impact of millions of new Great Commission-minded businessmen and women being raised up in the nations! What if even a portion of God's people learned to steward and generate finances for the Kingdom? The spiritual and economic benefits to the Church around the world would be off the charts. I have the privilege of

There is no place like the marketplace to show off the splendor and glory of Almighty God!

ministering to thousands of business leaders in the developing world. Most of the time, I take Christian businesspersons with me from the United States to serve as teachers and encouragers. Each time I go to an underserved country, I'm astounded by the hunger, receptivity, and eagerness to learn godly principles as they relate to business. I'm overwhelmed, not just by the needs, but also by the business opportunities that exist in these nations. What will it take to see spiritual and economic transformation in these needy nations?

First, it's going to take thousands of courageous, Spirit-filled entrepreneurs who are willing to do business in the developing world.

Second, it's going to take time. God is stirring the hearts of a multitude of businesspersons who want their lives and efforts to count for a larger purpose. Your greatest fulfillment, exhilaration, adventure, and purpose awaits you if you will dive into the global Great Commission.

No matter what line of business you're in, you have a role to play in God's ultimate business — the fulfilling of the Great Commission and the global honoring of His Son. Begin to ask God how He can use your business gifts to make both a local and global impact.

DAY_____DATE_____

DAILY PLANNER

Remember: *"Ask of me, and I will make the nations your inheritance, the ends of the earth your possession"* (Psalm 2:8; NIV).

Reflect: David Livingstone believed an entire continent could be transformed through "Christianity, commerce, and civilization." How can these components be used today for the transformation of nations?

Pray: For a new army of Great Commission-minded business leaders in every nation.

Act: What is your role in God's global plan to glorify His Son? Do something today to fulfill the role God has given you in His plan.

15

Great Commission Commerce

Today's world of globalization, ease of travel, and advanced technology provides Christians in business the greatest opportunity in history to extend God's Kingdom internationally. Businesspersons who love God are well-positioned to become the greatest-ever missions force in the world. Imagine the impact that could be made for God's Kingdom if Christ-honoring businesses led by Christ-honoring men and women were established in every nation! Kingdom business leaders can impact people and nations spiritually and economically.

Those of us in more advanced nations need to be reminded that we can play a major role in the global Great Commission. We can help our brothers and sisters in underserved nations become co-catalysts with us for fulfilling God's purposes for our time. Millions of Christian businesspersons in less developed, yet emerging economies are crying for us to help them gain the skills, knowledge, and ability to capture economic and spiritual opportunities in their nations.

You can play a significant role! Here are several things you can do, starting today.

You can help businesspersons in underserved nations embrace a biblical worldview. It's vital that we help businesspersons in the developing world see the world through a biblical lens that will shape their business practices. They need to know they are important and strategic in God's Kingdom. So often it takes outside affirmation for Christian businesspersons in severely challenged economies to truly see their significance. In *God is at Work*, Ken Eldred shows how vital a "spiritual capital account" is for any nation.[1] The spiritual capital account is the sum of all individual business transactions in a given nation, whether done with honesty or deceit. The sum total of each business deal and transaction is a nation's "spiritual capital." When marketplace Christians look at their world in these terms it puts things in a different light. We are responsible for the good of our communities, nation, and world. Christians must lead by example and spur others on to love and good works.[2]

You can mentor others. Effective Christian businesspersons in the developed world have so much to offer to businesspersons in developing nations. We can share our personal experiences and teach business strategies that have been proven over time. Practical teaching regarding budgeting, accounting, marketing, management principles, and employee relations can have a huge impact. My friend, Jim, is a business consultant who had a successful 30-year career at EDS in Dallas. Jim accompanied me twice to India and had a heart-connection with two Indian businessmen. For almost two years they have e-mailed each other every week. These Indian businessmen seek Jim's counsel on a variety of business and personal issues. Jim has expressed how rewarding it is to be making a difference in the lives of these Indian entrepreneurs.

Dawson Trotman, founder of the Navigators, would challenge every growing Christian to pour his or her life into a younger believer. His constant challenge was, "Where's your man? Where's your woman?" This is the principle of multiplication Paul gave Timothy.[3]

You can invest in legitimate projects. When you find a trustworthy person in a nation that has the knowledge, skills, and plan for a legitimate business project that can bless others, you may prayerfully consider becoming an investor. Obviously, each scenario carries its own set of risks, motivations, and possibilities. Nevertheless, one of the key ways businesspersons from the West can substantially bless a nation is to do business in that nation. Also, well-placed micro-loans to deserving, motivated recipients can yield huge dividends for God's purposes.

My friend Jeff has frequently visited Ghana for seven years. He has developed a heart for Ghana, along with a growing understanding of the complex economic, social, and spiritual issues at work in that nation. Now Jeff enjoys relationships with quality business and government leaders from various sectors of Ghana's economy. Jeff is taking American businessmen to Africa to explore various investment opportunities. These Ghana-based businesses will bless both the Church and the communities of that nation.

You can pray for and support ministries that are doing good work. God has blessed us to help support and come alongside various efforts that are promoting His work worldwide. Partnering with high integrity, effective ministries is much more than a responsibility; it's a privilege.

You can start where you are by mentoring those within your sphere of influence. Not everyone can travel internationally, but we have opportunities all around us every day. Start there. My friend Matt works with Ford Credit. Matt's heart was burdened to mentor fellow workers within the company in the Christian faith. He stepped out in faith and has seen God do things beyond his wildest expectations. Today, there are over 300 Ford employees in the group he started called Ford Employees for Christ. They meet in chapters and have regular conference calls to discuss inter-company issues and encourage one another in the Lord. Each person in the group aims to disciple at least one other person in the workplace over the course of the next year. They're already thinking in terms of supernatural multiplication!

Steve, in Indiana, is a successful entrepreneur with considerable executive experience. He has started several niche businesses that have prospered. Steve's passion is to disciple other men in the marketplace for Christ. He specifically seeks out young entrepreneurs who have a dream and a good business idea. He invests time with them through friendship, Bible study, prayer, and business strategy formulation. Steve is impacting lives by giving his time and heart to others. Some of the people he discipled are now repeating the process with other emerging leaders.

God stands ready to use your life for Great Commission commerce. You can help change lives and change nations.

DAY_____DATE_____

DAILY PLANNER

Remember: *"And the things that you have heard from me among many witnesses, commit these to faithful men who will be able to teach others also"* (2 Timothy 2:2).

Reflect: "The promise of Christianity is the joy and power of an integrated life; transformed on every level by the Holy Spirit, so that our whole being participates in the great drama of God's plan of redemption." — Nancy Pearcey[4]

Pray: Ask God for revelation concerning how He wants to use your life and business to impact others and help fulfill the Great Commission.

Act: Find two or three people you can disciple, mentor, and encourage.

16

Healthy Partnerships

I love the old *Peanuts* comic strip where Lucy tells Linus to change the TV channel. "Why should I?" Linus retorts. Then Lucy clenches her fist and says, "These individual fingers aren't much, but like this they're an awesome force!" Cowering away, Linus asks, "Which channel would you like?"

There is awesome strength in healthy partnerships. The Bible says that one may chase a thousand but there is exponential power with two. They can potentially put ten thousand on the run![1]

Unity is powerful, but double vision can be deadly. Have you ever literally "seen double"? If you've been hit hard in sports or had an accident that temporarily impaired your vision, you know how frightening it can be. Foggy vision can be debilitating. It warps your perspective and ability to focus. Clear vision, on the other hand, is powerful. When entering into business partnerships, it is essential for you and your partner to be of one mind and pursue a shared, single purpose. Does this mean you have to agree on every little thing? No. But you had better be aligned on the major components of the business.

Scripture explicitly warns against being *"unequally yoked together with unbelievers."*[2] God's Word is clear that light and darkness don't mix. If you're in a binding relationship with a non-believer, don't expect him to act like a Christian. It's not his nature. It's wise to think long and hard (and pray even harder!) before entering into a business partnership with a non-believer. As with any partnership, it's important to clearly define expectations, consequences of actions, and parameters. While it is possible to function in a business relationship with a non-Christian, it demands alignment in strategic areas. Conversely, just being in business with a fellow believer does not necessarily mean you are equally yoked. Regrettably, some very dysfunctional, miserable, and failed business partnerships can be found among Christians.

When you enter into any agreement with someone, his or her habits, reputation, work ethics, and ideology will follow him or her into the partnership. That's why it is no small decision when choosing a business partner. It's very much like a marriage. When considering a business alignment, are there warning signs or red flags regarding whom we should link with? There are many, but for brevity let's look at two.

Beware of those who try to pressure you into quick decisions. If someone is trying to pressure you to make a major decision with the threat of you "losing out on the deal," typically that would be a "red flag" to run the other direction. One of the oldest sales tricks in the world is to pressure someone into a rush decision by diverting their attention to the gains they'll lose by not jumping in. Yet Scripture says there is safety in taking deliberate steps and seeking broad counsel.[3]

Beware of those who always talk a big game. Some people are all talk, but they can't show any substantive results. Don't waste time with people who have accomplished little but boast as if they can conquer the world. There are those who talk like only "home runs" are a success, and triples or doubles are of no value. People who talk like that are not living in reality. Ask the Holy Spirit to help you discern those who merely "talk the talk" of faith, and those who have a track record of what their faith has produced.

Oneness of purpose among business partners is essential if the business is to stay on the intended course. To truly walk together, there must be agreement.[4] There are several key points where alignment must occur.

Equally yoked partners are aligned concerning the *purpose* of their business. That's why it's almost always best for business partners to be fellow Christ-followers. For instance, if your heart is to use a portion of the profits for charitable giving but your partner does not share your desire, you've got a problem. As a Christian, you want the business to have a positive social impact beyond the bottom line of merely making money. But is this a core value of your partner, as well?

Alignment must occur within the overall *strategy*. Agreement on the major selling points of the business and where the bulk of time, energy, and resources will be expended is crucial. What are the agreed-upon "growth engines" for the entity that require the most fuel and funding? Are you in agreement on how to best fuel for growth?

Alignment must also occur at major leverage points of the *process*. Are you equally yoked concerning major hiring decisions? Who will manage what? From the marketing strategy to sales to the culture and values of the business, agreement among the key decision-makers is vital. Is there at least broad agreement regarding salaries, equipment, marketing tools, and staff development?

The best time to determine if a potential partnership is an "equal yoke" is during the dating process. Clarity of direction, expectations, strategy, culture, and compensation should be defined and put on paper. It has been well observed that "nothing is real until it's written." Any business law professor will tell you that. Verbally expressing hopes and expectations is the first step. Then put it in writing, revisiting the same issues. If there is solid agreement in core principles, then seek wise counsel, ask for confirmation from God through His Word, and look for the inner witness of peace to proceed.

What if you are already unequally yoked in a business relationship? The first step is realization and changing your expectations to meet the current reality. Then, be proactive and intentional in finding the common ground between you and your partner or partners. In a spirit of unity, humility, and grace, talk through some of your differences and concerns. Cover your partner and the situation in prayer and ask God to guide you in taking the right steps, whether this means a continuance or a severing of the partnership.

One final thought — even if partnerships dissolve, friendships can continue. It's work — but it's well worth it. Do your part to *"keep the unity of the Spirit in the bond of peace."*[5]

DAY_____DATE_____

DAILY PLANNER

Remember: *"Do not be unequally yoked together with unbelievers"* (2 Corinthians 6:14).

Reflect: There is incredible power in healthy partnerships. One horse can pull a 2-ton load. Two horses independently can pull 4 tons. But tied together they can pull 18 tons.

Pray: For God to direct you into proper business alignments.

Act: Review your business partnerships and alliances.

17

Hidden Heroes

"I want to make a difference in my nation through business." Those were the words spoken to me by a young entrepreneur in India named Solomon. Solomon works for a large, multi-national consulting firm, and he has also started his own IT business. God has placed a vision in his heart to be a great businessman for the glory of God. I have the opportunity to minister to thousands of business leaders in developing nations. Some of the most amazing people in the world are businessmen and women who are serving Christ in underserved nations. More than likely you'll never hear their stories, yet their lives are making an eternal impact. These marketplace ministers are committed to bringing the light of Christ into their spheres of influence.[1]

I'll never forget meeting Vera, from Cameroon. She's a witty, intelligent, and joyful woman with a God-sized vision for her nation. Vera is a magistrate attorney who has committed her life to helping bring justice to mistreated women in West Africa. She uses her law practice to share God's love and to show His power. Recently, word got out about her practice and a film crew followed her around, creating a documentary titled "Sisters in Law." The film has won several awards, including an award from the acclaimed Cannes Film Festival. Vera fearlessly demonstrates her faith in Christ through her work. God is using her to bring righteousness, justice, and integrity to the nation of Cameroon.

Lela is a businesswoman in Hyderabad, India, who is determined to make a difference. Her city of Hyderabad is full of contrasts. On one hand, it is prospering as new jobs are being created every day. Tall, beautiful office buildings are being built in the city's high-tech region. Yet in the shadows of a growing middle-class are millions of people suffering in the worst imaginable poverty. Both the emerging middle-class and those caught in systemic poverty desperately need a relationship with Christ.

Lela was one of the first to introduce beauty boutiques and clinics in Hyderabad. God has blessed her business. She now has locations throughout India, even extending to New York, Paris, and Dubai. She is able to minister to women through her work in the marketplace. The profits she makes are used to help bring schooling and meals to needy children. In addition, she has a television program where she shares the good news of Jesus Christ.

A businessman named Maxwell attended our Global Advance Marketplace Conference for business leaders in Hyderabad. During a time for questions, an older, well-meaning Indian man stood up and declared it impossible to be a Christian and a businessperson in India. He said one must compromise and cheat to succeed. If you are a Christian and decide to do what is right, you will soon be out of business, he said. The crowd sat quiet and stunned for a few moments, until Maxwell stood up.

"I used to bribe," Maxwell said, "until I came to know Jesus."[2] Maxwell is in the concrete business and had placed his bid on a large job for the new airport. A group approached him to award him the contract, if he would agree to give them hidden bribes. He told them he would no longer practice bribes because he was now a follower of Jesus.

Maxwell lost what could easily have been his largest contract ever because of his stand for righteousness. He told us that for over six months he suffered financially but had inner peace, knowing he had obeyed the Lord. Months later he was again approached by the same group who had rejected his bid earlier because of his refusal to pay bribes. This time, things were different. God had honored Maxwell's integrity. The group told him they had been searching around, dealing with other contractors who could not be trusted. "We want you to have this job," they told Maxwell, "because you're the only person we trust." Not only did Maxwell get awarded the contract, he ended up getting twice the business originally discussed!

Then there's Rose from Kazakhstan. Rose invented a special bug repellent that has sold well in the retail markets of Almaty, the capital city. She was so excited to share with me. "I use my profits to help fund missions work in Afghanistan!" she told me. Here was a Kazakh entrepreneur using her talents and resources to bless another nation with the gospel!

Rose models a new kind of business entrepreneur, a Great Commission businessperson.[3] Here is a woman entrepreneur in a developing nation — and she is funding missions work to another underserved nation! She is a forerunner of many more Kingdom businesspersons who are even now emerging in those regions we once called the Third World. God is moving on the hearts of businesspersons all over the world. He can and will use anyone with a willing heart to serve Him and build His Kingdom.

DAY_____DATE_____

DAILY PLANNER

Remember: *"Then you will look and be radiant, your heart will throb and swell with joy; the wealth on the seas will be brought to you, to you the riches of the nations will come"* (Isaiah 60:5; NIV).

Reflect: God is granting an anointing for business to committed Christians worldwide. What can you do to proactively meet some Christian entrepreneurs from other nations?

Pray: For Kingdom-minded businesspersons in every nation.

Act: Find a committed, Christian entrepreneur in an underserved nation you can encourage.

18

History Lesson

*W*hen I was growing up, there was a clear inference that you had to be "in the ministry" if you really wanted to serve God and honor Him. And "in the ministry" invariably meant you were some kind of preacher. Unfortunately, remnants of this unscriptural dichotomy exist to this day. I've even heard people say, "Oh, sure, you can sort of serve God as a businessman, but if you *really* want to serve Him, you'd better be a preacher." Where I grew up we even had a name for it — *surrendering* to the ministry. This twisted mindset was something akin to a Wild West showdown: "Okay, now come out with your hands up! I know you're in there in the marketplace, thriving in your job and feeling a deep sense of accomplishment. And I know you're salt, light, and an agent for real transformation, but it's time to get out of that evil place and do some real work for the Lord. Hope you enjoyed making all that money, because now you're going in the ministry, so kiss the finer things of life goodbye." No wonder they called it surrendering!

People weren't taught that their present jobs *are* the arena of ministry where God has called them. Instead of being missionaries in the marketplace, too many Christians have pined to get out of the "sinful environment" of their workplaces. God sent them to those places as witnesses of the gospel and as change agents. But they had been taught that, because they were businesspersons, they were not "in the ministry."

The tragedies this unscriptural thinking has brought to some families are real. I saw some young men in seminary who frankly couldn't preach their way out of a paper bag — but they were awesome businessmen! Yet they had uprooted their families, believing that they had to be "in the ministry" to take their next step of obedience to God. How sad that most of them, in leaving their businesses, were exiting the most fruitful ministry they would ever have.

All of this has deep historical roots. Let's go way back. Most of the Greek philosophers taught a dualistic view of life. There was the physical world — that's where people lived and interacted in business, education, science, and government. Then there was the metaphysical world — religion, values, and virtues. There was perceived to be a thick black line between these two realms. This unscriptural, "two-tiered" worldview remains very much alive. In fact, it is the dominant worldview in our culture. It produces politicians who can say with a straight face, "Well, my personal belief is that abortion is wrong. But that's just part of my value system [the metaphysical realm]. I would never let my personal values determine the way I vote [the physical realm]."

A two-tiered businessperson might convince himself, "I know I ought to tell the truth [the metaphysical realm], but I want this contract, so I'm going to inflate the numbers [the physical realm]." Then, to salve his guilty conscience, he might even make a feeble attempt to reconcile these conflicting loyalties: "God knows I'm trying to provide for my family, so He understands if I stretch the truth a little."

If your thinking has been affected by this truncated view of life — let the truth set you free![1] You've been viewing life through a lens that has been adopted from a pagan, though highly intellectual, ancient Greek culture. It was reinforced by Constantine when an unholy fusion of church and state accommodated split loyalties. Some Protestant reformers, notably John Calvin, pounded away at this falsehood, insisting that, for the loyal follower of Christ, there is no fence between *secular* and *sacred*. All of life is to be viewed as sacred — as both stewardship and worship to God.[2] Still, this distorted, dualistic way of looking at life continues to pollute the Church.

The marketplace is often viewed as carnal because it deals with physical, earthly things like business or money. At best, the marketplace is often viewed as some kind of neutral zone where our faith has little if anything to say about affecting systems of economics, treatment of workers, or the great social issues of our time. Christians continue to be urged toward the inner, "spiritual" realities, while letting the "real world" take its natural course. Too many Christians are content to just let Jesus clean up the mess of the real world when He returns. But this dishonors His redemptive work. If Jesus turns individuals into a new creation,[3] does it not follow that we, as transformed persons, are His agents to transform culture? Jesus died to redeem us so that we, as His ambassadors, might be redemptive agents in the world. As Christ-followers, we have received both a Great Commission[4] *and* a cultural mandate.[5] Our great need today is a biblical worldview and a biblical world vision.

God gave the very first job description when He said, *"Be fruitful and multiply; fill the earth and subdue it."*[6] To "be fruitful and multiply" means to develop the social world: build families, churches, schools, cities, governments, laws. To "subdue the earth" means we are to harness the natural world: plant crops, build infrastructures, design computers, compose music. Our original purpose was (and still is) to create cultures and build civilizations — cooperating with God and for His glory.

All of life is to be integrated under the unrivaled lordship of Jesus Christ. The motto of Wheaton College is "For Christ and His Kingdom." The motto of my alma mater, John Brown University, is "Christ Over All." These are not just great slogans, this the way we are to live. God the Father has placed His Son at the center of everything: *"All things were created through Him and for Him. And He is before all things, and in Him all things consist. And He is the head of the body, the church . . . that in all things He may have the preeminence."*[7] Wherever we are, whatever we're doing — it is for Christ and His Kingdom.[8] He is indeed over *all.*

DAY_____DATE_____

DAILY PLANNER

Remember: *"The earth is the Lord's, and all its fullness, the world and those who dwell therein"* (Psalm 24:1).

Reflect: "We are involved in bringing the Creator's work to its intended fulfillment by being co-creators in a very grand project, indeed." — Michael Novak[9]

Pray: For an integrated, biblical worldview where all of life is lived to God's glory.

Act: Demonstrate your faith today in a tangible way in the marketplace. See yourself as an agent sent by God to transform culture. Erase the unscriptural line between faith and practice.

19
Prayer and the Workplace

You have a powerful business advantage — you can connect with heaven. But, are you *taking advantage of your advantage*?

Many businesspersons don't capitalize on this awesome privilege because, in their minds, they're just too busy to pray. If you feel that way — and we've all been there at some point — let me encourage you with a few reminders.

First, if you will give God the firstfruits of your day, He will work with time in your behalf. Remember, since God created time He can manipulate it for His purposes — and for your benefit. God literally made time stand still so Joshua could fulfill his God-given assignment, and so that His purposes would prevail. This gift of extra time was a direct answer to Joshua's prayer.[1]

Martin Luther, who knew a thing or two about pressure, famously said he was so busy that he could not get it all done without spending two hours each day in prayer. And John Wesley, who also established a worldwide movement, said in a matter-of-fact way, "God does nothing but in answer to prayer."[2]

Second, remember the cost that made your hotline to heaven possible. The moment Jesus died, something astounding happened across town. The curtain in the temple that had separated the people from God's presence was dramatically ripped from the top to the bottom.[3] God did it. Talk about a helpful visual aid! God was demonstrating in no uncertain terms that access into His presence was now possible for *everyone, at any time!* Not just the religious professionals, and not just once a year.

Prayer is a summit meeting at the very highest level; this summit takes place in the very throne room of the universe. And you have direct access.

But access to God has only one password; we can only come to God through His Son, Jesus Christ.[4] May we never forget the enormous cost — it cost Jesus His life to throw open the doors for us to have immediate access to God.[5] Now we come without fear into God's presence and boldly make our requests known.[6] So pray big prayers. Phillips Brooks said, "You cannot think a prayer so large that God, in answering it, will not wish you had made it larger."[7]

Third — and this should lift your hopes — most history-shaping prayers were short. The importance is not in length but focus and intensity. In fact, Jesus warned against what He called *"vain repetition"* in prayer.[8] Remember, *"the effective, fervent prayer of a righteous man avails much."*[9]

Finally, here are some practical, short prayers you can pray throughout the day. These short, focused prayers can be shot heavenward straight from your desk at work. Each prayer is directly from Scripture, so you know you are praying in God's will.

- **A Prayer of Focus.** Commonly referred to as the Lord's Prayer, this prayer will focus your day on God's Kingdom, power, and glory.[10]

- **A Prayer of Increase.** This famous prayer of Jabez invites God's blessing and expansion on your life and work.[11]

- **A Prayer for Boldness.** When the early Church got its first taste of persecution, they responded by praying for boldness to proclaim Christ and minister in supernatural power. They received what they requested and were filled with the Holy Spirit.[12]

- **A Prayer for Unity.** Christ's intercessory prayer for the spiritual unity of His followers should be echoed by every disciple. This prayer for unity has a distinctly evangelistic purpose, *"that the world may believe that You sent Me."*[13]

- **The Prayers of Paul.** Peppered through each of his letters, these prayers, when personalized, yield dramatic spiritual results.

- **A Prayer of Influence.** I often call this "the businessperson's prayer." It is a prayer for covenant blessing, again with an evangelistic intent, *"that Your way may be known on earth, Your salvation among all nations."*[14]

- **A Prayer of Enablement.** At those times when challenges seem insurmountable, we should take a cue from Zerubbabel and cry out for God's grace — His Spirit's enablement and intervention. This is a powerful, single word prayer of declaration.[15]

- **A Prayer of Assurance.** Technically not a prayer, this is a refocusing in God's presence where we recall once again who is truly in control. *"Be still, and know that I am God; I will be exalted among the nations, I will be exalted in the earth!"*[16]

You're not just working for a company; you are working with God, and your joint-agenda is strategic. The apostle Paul says we are *"God's fellow workers."*[17] Through prayer, we are working with God to affect the outcome of history. We are partnering with Him to determine the future! Paul Billheimer, in his classic book, *Destined for the Throne*, called prayer "on the job training" for our future ruling in Christ's Kingdom. We learn now to defeat Satan and his demon forces through prayer.[18]

J. Sidlow Baxter was right: "Men may spurn our appeals, reject our message, oppose our arguments, despise our persons — but they are helpless against our prayers."[19]

DAY_____DATE_____

DAILY PLANNER

Remember: *"Call to Me, and I will answer you, and show you great and mighty things, which you do not know"* (Jeremiah 33:3).

Reflect: "The Bible pray-ers prayed as if their prayers could and would make an objective difference. The apostle Paul gladly announces that we are 'co-laborers with God'; that is, we are working with God to determine the outcome of events (1Cor. 3:9). We are working with God to determine the future! Certain things will happen in history if we pray rightly. We are to change the world by prayer."
— Richard J. Foster[20]

Pray: That you will give prayer its proper place in your life each day.

Act: Start today, by praying these short, suggested prayers.

20

Prospering from Problems

We all love to claim the promises of Jesus. But there is one of His sure-fire promises that needs no claiming: In this life you will have problems.[1] If the Lord said it, you can take that one to the bank. Business is a breeding ground for problems. The moment you start working and dealing with people, egos, ideas, and resources, you will encounter problems. There's no getting around it. One of the thorns we must live with is the fact that sin exists and influences even the best-intentioned people. Any shrewd manager should expect nothing less in his planning. So it's wise to calculate "buffer space" in your planning process that takes into account incompetence, inefficiencies, lies, selfishness, and greed. Of course, we should expect the best from our business associates. But we cannot buy in to the unscriptural notion that people are "basically good." The Bible teaches that we are all tainted by sin and outside of Christ's redemptive work, our natural state is tilted toward deceit.[2]

Therefore, bad things just happen. The reasons are varied, but sin has colored our human condition. Added to this, we sometimes make the wrong call on issues. Unlike God, we are not omniscient, and the holes in our knowledge often work against us. As a follower of Christ, you can expect times when you will be in the devil's cross hairs; demonic attacks will seek to derail your God-sent assignment. If today you find yourself under spiritual attack, take heart. You're probably doing something right!

People are never the real problem. The Bible says *"we do not wrestle against flesh and blood, but against principalities, against powers, against the rulers of the darkness of this age, against spiritual hosts of wickedness in the heavenly places."*[3] We can stand in victory against the attacks of the enemy by putting on the armor of God.[4] As a Kingdom businessperson, you should enlist intercessors to cover you and your business in prayer. Still, many times God allows us to go through difficulties. Through these problems God tests and develops our character. Overcoming problems helps us prosper now and in eternity. When viewed with an eternal perspective, our current problems are whittled down to their appropriate size, and we realize they are not permanent.[5] The old adage is true: "This too shall pass."

What is your attitude when problems arise? I love entrepreneurs who see problems as opportunities. That's really what they are. Problems are opportunities for us to grow. Pressures and difficulties are opportunities to learn and mature, while applying God's principles into the pressing situation. When you think about it, most business, at its essence, is about solving problems. Businesses create products and services that answer a problem or need. Commerce creates an opportunity for us to instill God's creativity into providing a solution. His Spirit gives us the fortitude to press on during the most difficult of circumstances.[6] God wants to partner with us in the problem by bringing Him into the situation. When God shows up, things change. We need to view problems as blessings in the long run. Problems can help you grow into a more fruitful, competent steward in your marketplace ministry. Once you've proven you can shoulder problems with grace, you will receive greater respect, authority, and a deeper insight. Businesses recognize people who can bring solutions to the table. As you grow in problem-solving abilities, you earn the right and authority to speak into situations.

If you're going through a difficult situation, cry out to God to meet you there.[7] Ask for His grace to grow and mature. He's getting you in shape so you can play ball at a more advanced level.

DAY_____DATE_____

DAILY PLANNER

Remember: *"In this world you will have trouble. But take heart! I have overcome the world"* (John 16:33; NIV).

Reflect: Problems are a gymnasium to get us in shape to function effectively at a higher level.

Pray: For the right attitude and perspective when problems arise.

Act: Invite God's presence and participation in solving your problems. Trust Him today for heaven-sent solutions.

21

Right Thinking

Henry Ford often quipped, "If you think you can, or you think you can't — you're right."[1]

One of the greatest factors in determining our success in life is our mental disposition. Our state of mind, whether positive or negative, will greatly determine how high we will soar in life and business. Some people say, "You are what you eat." While there is some truth to that, the Bible clearly teaches that we are what we *think*.[2]

Having the correct mindset is a must. We should ask each day for the mind of Christ. God's Word urges, *"Let God transform you into a new person by changing the way you think."*[3] Elephants are arguably the world's strongest and largest animals. A common technique is used by trainers to keep elephants confined to one place. The trainer ties a rope to the elephant's tail and stakes the rope into the ground. This little trick keeps elephants contained. But how? When the elephant is small the trainer ties its tail to the stake. The young elephant tries time after time to break free, but he can't. At some point in the young elephant's mind, he decides to stop trying to break free. Elephants are known for acute memories. As the elephant grows larger and stronger, he has no idea of his own strength. The trainer continues to use the trick of the rope and stake. The mindset of the elephant and his memory of past failure keep the animal constrained and unaware of his potential.

Many of us are like the elephants. We have mental blockades that have held us back from reaching our full potential. Each of us must blast through mental barriers that affect our attitudes. There are many "brain blockades" but let's focus on a few. Note first the barrier of *discouragement*. We're commanded regularly in Scripture not to be discouraged, although it is so easy to be so. Almost every great hero of the faith had to battle seasons of discouragement. Think of the discouragement Job battled when he lost everything. From Joseph to David, to Paul and to Peter — they all faced times of deep discouragement.

The etymology of *discourage* is interesting. Often God exhorted Joshua to *"be of good courage."* When we are discouraged we become "dis-couraged." If we give in to discouragement, it's like taking the wind out of our sails. Courage collapses when we are sullen. If you've been in business more than a day, or have had a pulse long enough, no doubt you've faced discouragement. Perhaps you had high hopes for a transaction or business opportunity that fell through. Maybe you've committed everything to the Lord and are working with all your might, yet it still seems impossible to get traction in your business. Perhaps someone you really depended on let you down in a major way. Don't let discouragement and disappointment keep you down. A good antidote to discouragement is to meditate on God's faithfulness to you in the past[4] and Christ's sure victory in the future.[5]

Another common blockade to a God-honoring mindset is *failure*. Every great leader and successful business person has experienced failure to some degree. We need to see failure with the correct mentality. Failure can teach us things about ourselves, about God, and about our ministry in the marketplace. Thomas Edison had a healthy attitude toward failure. After thousands of unsuccessful attempts at creating an electric light bulb he said, "If I find 10,000 ways something won't work, I haven't failed. I am not discouraged, because every wrong attempt discarded is another step forward."[6] Pursuit of vision, ideas, and dreams requires tenacity and the attitude to grow and learn from our failures.

Believe it or not, *success* can also be a powerful enemy to right thinking. Why? Because if success is not processed properly, it can breed pride and lethargy.

Many people are desperate for God when the chips are down. But when fortune comes, they forsake Him. George MacDonald understood the land mines placed in the way of the successful when he observed, "Without Christ a man must fail miserably, or succeed even more miserably."[7] Will you honor and remember God when he grants you success and the accolades of people? *"The crucible for silver, the furnace for gold, but man is tested by the praise he receives."*[8]

How will you handle the success test? Success can play with your head, making you think you are the one who deserves credit rather than God. If we're not vigilant, humble, and grateful, success can lull us into pride and a false confidence. Too much success too fast can distort our view of reality concerning our business. When the Internet was new, CompuServe was one of the first companies to offer users online navigation and accounts. They dominated the market for years, paying little attention to other start-ups who were offering similar services. But slowly, over time, AOL and other companies became serious competitors, offering cheaper prices and better options to customers. CompuServe failed to act quickly because their huge success had bred false security. Today they only have a small percentage of the market.

Of course, the most spectacular "computer" of all is between your ears. What input are you logging into your magnificent mind? The Bible teaches that we are to condition our minds with intentional thoughts that are noble, just, pure, lovely, uplifting, virtuous, and praiseworthy.[9] Your attitude will determine your altitude. Recalibrate your mind to God's truth and let Him train you to think right about business, about life.

DAY_____DATE_____

DAILY PLANNER

Remember: *"Do not conform any longer to the patterns of this world, but be transformed by the renewing of your mind"* (Romans 12:2; NIV).

Reflect: "You will remain young as long as you are open to what is beautiful, good, and great, receptive to the messages of other men and women, of nature and of God. If one day you should become bitter, pessimistic, and gnawed by despair, may God have mercy on your old man's soul." — Douglas MacArthur[10]

Pray: For God to give you the right mindset regarding your life's circumstances.

Act: No matter how difficult your situation may be today, make the necessary attitude adjustments.

22

Righteous Risk-taking

*S*uccess requires risks. In life, business, and relationships, we must risk if we want to advance. Nothing substantial is accomplished without risking. I (Jonathan) remember the first time I met Sarah, the woman who is now my wife. She was so beautiful, but I was hesitant and afraid to talk to her. What if she rejected me? What if I stumbled over my words? What if I looked stupid and made a fool of myself? I was scared! But it's much more frightening now to think how different my life would be had I not dared to risk. Thank God, I gathered the nerve to talk to her. We developed a friendship and married a year later.

Learning from people who have acquired wisdom through the years is something I love to do. I often ask them what they wish they would have done differently. Many of them say, "I wish I would have risked more." That's an interesting and profound answer! If we know risk is essential to growth and advancement, then why don't we risk more? Fear of failure is one of the biggest reasons. Fear often holds us back from reaching our full potential. A great question to ponder is this: *What could I accomplish if I had no fear?* That's one to chew on for a while.

Inordinate fear certainly does not come from God. He has not given us a spirit of timidity. On the contrary, he has given us the spirit of power, love, and sound judgment.[1] His good word to you today is, *"Fear not, for I am with you; be not dismayed, for I am your God. I will strengthen you, yes, I will help you, I will uphold you with My righteous right hand."*[2]

What is holding you back from going to the next level? Why not break out today and ask to schedule a meeting with the client of your dreams? Why not present your idea or project to those you have considered out of your league? Yes, going to the next level will require uncomfortable risks and the potential of failure. So what if you fail? Each time you step out and push beyond the zones of comfort and convenience, you grow and mature.

Our God is a big God, and He is good. He wants to bless you. His favor can open doors and move mountains on your behalf.[3] God is moved by your faith.[4] It pleases Him.[5] He will meet you as you step out in faith and take action. You must risk to be great and to accomplish great things. There is no getting around it. God meets us in our place of discomfort. He commanded Joshua to step boldly into unknown territory, and He is calling you do to the same.[6]

Many great orators had to get over an initial fear of public speaking. Great athletes have to learn to perform under pressure and before large crowds. Heroes of the Bible dared to obey God when all odds were stacked against them. Are you risking righteously? True entrepreneurs take risks and discern opportunities. Michael Novak observes, "Entrepreneurs often see a little more in humble things than other people do. Their characteristic habit is sharp discernment."[7]

At the same time, we must avoid foolish risks. We are warned not to test God by presumptuous acts.[8] God has put natural laws in place. If you go a week without sleep you will crash and burn. If you jump off a ten-story building you will have a serious encounter with the law of gravity. No person in his right mind would jump from a high place thinking God would suspend His natural laws and somehow prevent them from harm. This is a trick the devil tried on Jesus when He was tempted in the wilderness, but Jesus wasn't fooled.[9] If the Son of God respected God's natural laws, we should too.

Yet in terms of business, many Christians jump off of ten-story buildings every day. They make bad agreements, enter unwise partnerships, and launch untested projects — all in the name of "faith." Jesus talked about counting the cost before diving into a project. Jesus told of a man who dove into a project of building a tower without proper planning and considerations. In the end, he was unable to finish the job and was ridiculed and his reputation was ruined.[10] Nobody bats 1.000 in business decisions. But business persons can call on God's wisdom to discern a bad risk or, a right time to move forward with prudent action.[11]

How can you know when to risk and when to go the conservative, conventional route? God gives us several guideposts to aid us in decisions.

1. What does God's Word say pertaining to your particular situation? Is there Scripture that correlates to your business process, idea, or opportunity?

2. What is wise counsel telling you? Seek wise, experienced people who want to see you succeed and ask for their input. Be open to what they say, then weigh their counsel in your own heart and spirit. Someone in our lives who can see our blind spots is a true gift from God. Trusted friends and advisors may be able to discern coming hazards that you had not considered. On the flip side, they may perceive that you need nudging to *risk* your way to the next level of growth and productivity.

3. Have you done your homework? Have you researched, crunched numbers, and considered multiple scenarios and outcomes? What is the absolute worst that could happen? If you lost every penny, could you sleep at night with peace? What would it look like if you only hit 25 percent of your projections? Is it worth the time, energy, and effort? Practicing genuine faith also means you are willing to face brutal reality head-on.

4. What is the Holy Spirit revealing to you? If you stay connected to the true vine, Jesus Christ, He will direct you and make you fruitful.[12] If the Holy Spirit is prompting you to take a risk, obey His prompting. If He is cautioning you to hold off, obey His inner directive. There will come a point where you will just know. As a maturing son or daughter of God through faith in Christ, you can expect Him to lead you.[13]

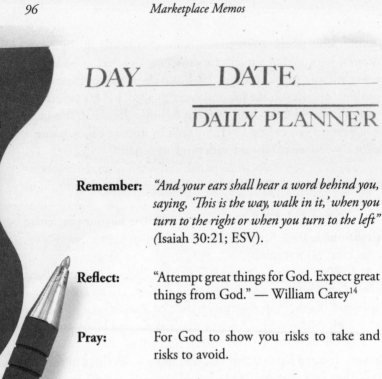

DAY_____ DATE_____

DAILY PLANNER

Remember: *"And your ears shall hear a word behind you, saying, 'This is the way, walk in it,' when you turn to the right or when you turn to the left"* (Isaiah 30:21; ESV).

Reflect: "Attempt great things for God. Expect great things from God." — William Carey[14]

Pray: For God to show you risks to take and risks to avoid.

Act: Seek wise counsel for upcoming decisions.

23

Seeds

Y ou cannot be fruitful if you do not sow seeds. All nature proves it: you cannot bear fruit if you do not plant seeds. That's why Jesus taught that seed-sowing is an essential part of following Him. *"By this My Father is glorified,"* He said, *"that you bear much fruit; so you will be My disciples."* [1]

Fruitfulness is the natural, healthy result of seed-sowing. Sowing and reaping is an irrevocable, universal law. As the great preacher Charles Spurgeon said, "Seedtime and harvest are tied together in a sure knot." [2]

This was dramatically illustrated in a little-known story of two young men who would later lead powerhouse evangelical ministries. One night in the mid-1940s, a young college graduate was thumbing a ride to Los Angeles. (Sixty years ago, this was safe.) Not yet a Christian, his goal in life was to become a millionaire and live in Beverly Hills.

A man picked up the young hitchhiker and they began to talk. "Do you know anywhere in Los Angeles I can spend the night?" the traveler inquired. "I think so," replied the driver. "There's a guy named Dawson Trotman who's feeding some sailors at his house, teaching them the Bible or something. Maybe he'd find you a bed tonight."

And so it was that, on his first night in California, young Bill Bright received Dawson Trotman's hospitality. Little did either of them realize that within a few years they would both lead large, influential ministries.

A decade after that sovereign night, Trotman's Navigators were in a race against time to purchase Glen Eyrie, their proposed Colorado headquarters. Bill Bright, by now founder of the fledgling Campus Crusade for Christ, personally gave sacrificially and wrote 5,000 friends of his new organization, asking them to help. With Bright's help, the Navigators were able to purchase the property.[3]

Little did Dawson Trotman realize that one night's room and board, given in Jesus' name, would yield thousands of dollars when it was needed most. Dawson Trotman and Bill Bright, early in their ministries, had tapped into an eternal principle — *seeds sown will multiply and bear fruit.*

As far as eternal life is concerned, the Bible teaches there are only two kinds of people — saved and lost. But as far as *this* world is concerned there are also two kinds of people. First, there are the vast majority who intrinsically feel that the world owes them something. Then there are those wonderful people who intrinsically feel they owe the world something. It is this select group who are history makers. History makers are seed sowers. The apostle Paul was in the second category. He felt he owed the world the gospel.[4] What do you feel you owe the world?

Here are some thoughts about seeds and fruitfulness.

1. God gives seeds, not for eating but for sowing. So, don't eat your seed! Don't consume yourself what can be sown for others and for God's Kingdom. Only *planted* seeds experience the miracle of multiplication. Jesus said, *"Unless a grain of wheat falls into the ground and dies, it remains alone; but if it dies it produces much grain."*[5]

2. Seeds sown in faith *will* multiply. A couple of kernels of planted seed corn will produce a stalk of several ears. And each ear will contain hundreds of seed kernels (403, on average, to be precise). Our God of abundance has structured life on this earth so that the fruitfulness from seeds is always far greater than the seeds themselves. Do you believe that? Are you practicing that? Are you sowing good seed, expecting a harvest? Nate Wolf observes, "If you want multiplication in your business, you must first put multiplication in your eyes, ears, and mouth." Get in sync with God — *expect* a high return on seed you sow.

3. Good seeds are almost indestructible, and one seed in particular never dies. You were born physically by the implanting of a seed. Also, you are born again spiritually by receiving the good seed of the gospel. This seed of God's Word is literally incorruptible. It lives forever.[6] Be careful to sow *good* seed, because you will reap what you sow. If you sow to your own desires, you will be consumed by those desires. But if you sow to what is eternal, you will *"reap everlasting life."*[7]

What seeds will you sow today? If you will commit to sow seed, God will ensure you have seed to sow. God *"supplies seed to the sower."*[8] Notice that God promises to supply seed to sowers — those who will scatter seed for the betterment of people and the furtherance of God's Kingdom. As we learn to sow and give generously, we experience God's promise of a sure return.[9] Jesus taught that giving always beats receiving.[10] Winston Churchill was right when he observed, "We make a living by what we get, but we make a life by what we give." Ask any farmer: sowing seed is an intentional activity. So look for opportunities today to sow seed.

I once spoke at a Bible school in Africa that had a great motto: *I will find a way, every day, to give something to God and something to people.* There are many kinds of seeds and many opportunities to sow them. Every day you have opportunity to sow seeds — seeds of kindness, inspiration, money, time, prayer, faith, hope, and love. You want to have much fruit to lay at Jesus' feet. That will demand that you sow much seed — intentionally, everyday. God is glorified when your life bears much fruit. But God has a system for fruit-bearing. You cannot bear much fruit unless you sow much seed. So, don't eat your seed. Don't be stingy with your seed. *Scatter* your seed, and God will give you more. *"One man gives freely yet gains even more; another withholds unduly, but comes to poverty. A generous man will prosper; he who refreshes others will himself be refreshed."*[11]

DAY_____DATE_____

DAILY PLANNER

Remember: *"He who sows sparingly will also reap sparingly, and he who sows bountifully will also reap bountifully. So let each one give as he purposes in his heart, not grudgingly or of necessity, for God loves a cheerful giver"* (2 Corinthians 9:6–7).

Reflect: "Success is knowing your purpose in life, growing to reach your maximum potential, and sowing seeds that benefit others." — John Maxwell[12]

Pray: That you will be perceptive and responsive to daily opportunities to sow seeds that will yield much fruit for Christ and His Kingdom.

Act: What will you give today to God? What will you give today to others?

24

Strong Relationships

My dad's pastor when he was a young man was a wise, visionary named O.W. Webb. Pastor Webb gave younger pastors this sage counsel: "No one enters your life by accident. Either he is there for you to minister to him, or for him to minister to you."

Almost everything in business is based on relationships. Relationships are central to your dealings with clients, suppliers, vendors, partners, employees, and contractors. There is so much that can be said regarding relationships and the role they play in business. Every single product or service is created by people to be used by people. Relationships create the fabric of commerce.

Having healthy relationships with the right people may well be the single most important ingredient in success. I like this adage because it rings true: *"If I'm not networking, I'm not working."*

Effective leaders in business are always tending their network of relationships. They cultivate existing relationships and are intentional in meeting new people in their industry. Who is it that could benefit from your product or service? Who might have an interest in what you are doing? Who is God leading you to serve and bless? Relationships grow in two ways: by providence and by purpose. There are times when we just happen to be "at the right place at the right time." We meet someone new and a relationship begins. Most of the time, however, it is up to us to purposefully initiate contacts and build relationships. Even when we meet people providentially, it is up to us to follow up with them.

As your network grows, it becomes increasingly important — and more challenging — to manage and nurture your relationships. You will need a plan to systematically give attention to those in your network. Some in your network will require more regular contact and follow-up, while others will only require occasional contact. If you ask Him, God will help you develop the skill of stewarding multiple relationships, knowing how much attention should be given to each relationship. Some in your network have a natural leaning toward an "out of sight, out of mind" relationship. In these instances, to stay on their relational radar you should look for creative, memorable experiences that will create a bond between the two of you.

Another way to strengthen your relational base is to serve and meet the needs of those in your network. Many times, you will know people who can be of great benefit or help to others you know. By simply playing the role of a connector, you have done both persons a tremendous service. An important rule of thumb to apply in new relationships is to be quick to give. Look for ways to make a valuable deposit into the other person, not seeking anything in return. Because this is so against the norm, you will automatically distinguish yourself from others. God's way is always about giving and serving others.[1] So what are some keys to building a strong base of relationships?

- Be proactive in seeking people out.

- Go to strategic places where people in your field congregate.

- Follow up with those you meet.

- Have a system or file for your contacts and their information.

- Find ways to serve and care for those in your network.

- Systematically contact those in your network.

- Help connect people to others who can benefit them.

- Always be the first to give.

Christians are advantaged in relationships because our faith will never allow us to view anyone as an expendable object. Rather, Christians believe that all people — even those who oppose the gospel — are created in God's image, and simply because they are humans they are the crowning glory of His creation. Each life counts.[2] Further, God loves humans to the extent that He became one.[3] The eternal Son of God became the Son of Man and died to restore us to *relationship* with God.[4] Jesus taught us to love our neighbors as much as we love ourselves.[5]

The gospel spread initially through relationships. Here are just a few examples. Barnabas befriended Saul (later named Paul) and became his advocate to Church leaders who were suspect of him.[6] A tight-knit, racially diverse group of local Church leaders obeyed the Holy Spirit's directive and commissioned Barnabas and Saul to take the gospel to the unreached.[7] A businesswoman named Lydia met Paul, became the first convert to Christ in Macedonia, and helped him establish a beachhead for the gospel in Europe.[8] A physician named Luke accompanied Paul, assisting in keeping him healthy for his rigorous missionary journeys.[9] Paul formed a strong bond with Aquila and Priscilla, who shared his vocation of tent-making and were frequent travel and ministry companions.[10] Although the friendship of Peter and Paul was tested by an in-your-face theological confrontation, they remained friends and complemented each other's ministry.[11]

Three years ago I attended a luncheon by myself. I happened to sit next to a gentleman named Wayne. We struck up a great conversation. I told him about the work I'm involved in and listened intently to what his interests and work entailed. Wayne seemed to show genuine interest in my work so I invited him to a future event I was putting together. He accepted the invitation and came as my guest. Wayne's heart was stirred by the presentation. I followed up with him and we met several times for lunch in the ensuing months. Our relationship strengthened to the point where Wayne recently accompanied me on a trip to India to equip business leaders. Now he is working with me on future projects for India and here in the United States. In addition, we have introduced each other to a host of relationships that will prove to be mutually beneficial. I can truly say that Wayne has become a friend and someone I deeply respect. All of this came from following through with someone I happened to sit by at a luncheon. God honors the process of developing and stewarding relationships. Learn to value people and build strength in your relationships.

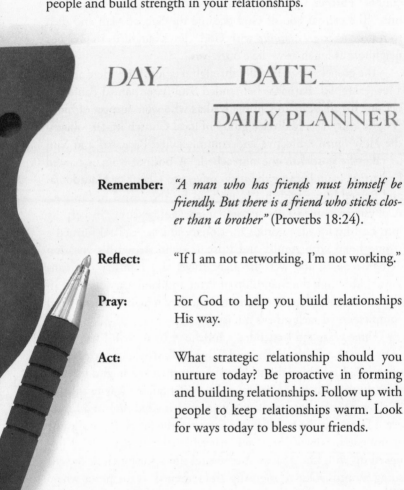

DAY_____ DATE_____

DAILY PLANNER

Remember: *"A man who has friends must himself be friendly. But there is a friend who sticks closer than a brother"* (Proverbs 18:24).

Reflect: "If I am not networking, I'm not working."

Pray: For God to help you build relationships His way.

Act: What strategic relationship should you nurture today? Be proactive in forming and building relationships. Follow up with people to keep relationships warm. Look for ways today to bless your friends.

The Fight of Your Life

If you're serious about enthroning Jesus in the workplace, God's got your number. And so does the devil.

There's a fast track to getting on the devil's hit list — get serious about advancing the Kingdom of God. When a person seriously commits to fulfilling the Great Commission, he will be in the devil's cross hairs. Of course, this does not mean we retreat from evangelism, missions, and transformation. It does mean we realize this is a real war with real casualties. And one of the greatest theaters of war is in the marketplace.

Through the years, I've heard many businesspersons who wanted to do something significant for the Kingdom say essentially the same thing — "What happened? My business and career were doing fine, but as soon as I really committed my work to God for His purposes, all hell broke loose!"

That's more than just an expression. All hell *does* break loose when you commit to being a Kingdom agent in the workplace. You are defying the right of Satan to operate unimpeded. In embracing the Kingdom and committing to its expansion, you announce to the enemy's camp your intention to dislodge his holdings and plant the rightful flag of Christ's Kingdom where the devil has — until you came along — operated with impunity. No wonder he's angry! The fact is, you've got a war on your hands. "Spiritual warfare" is not cute theological jargon; this is a real war with a real enemy, real casualties, and verifiable victories.

But don't be afraid and don't be intimidated. Jesus has already won the victory.[1] *"He who is in you is greater than he who is in the world."*[2] Nor should you think it's strange that the devil would attack you. God allows these *"fiery trials."* Through them you *"partake of Christ's sufferings, that when His glory is revealed, you may be glad with exceeding joy."*[3] And Christ's glory won't just be revealed when He returns to earth; He wants to reveal His glory through you — *now*. God wants you to rejoice as you see Jesus win in the marketplace!

The question, then, is how do you arm yourself for spiritual combat and victory? I urge you to take these clear steps to winning the fight of your life.

Repent immediately of all known sin. Keep short accounts with God. Allow no unconfessed sin in your life. When we confess and turn away from any and all sin, God's forgiveness is immediate.[4] Don't give the devil a foothold in your life through sin. Live under Christ's lordship; deny the enemy access into your life. *"Abstain from every form of evil."*[5]

Bracket your day with time in God's presence. The enemy cannot operate in an atmosphere permeated by God's Word, prayer, and worship.[6]

Be filled with the Spirit and walk in the Spirit. God's Holy Spirit gives us power over all the devil's schemes as we live under His control.[7] When we *"abide in the vine"* (Jesus), we are victorious and fruitful.[8]

Humble yourself daily before the Lord. All successful engaging of the enemy follows a simple pattern of submitting to God and resisting the attacks of the enemy.[9]

Establish true accountability with a trusted accountability partner. Real accountability with a trusted, godly friend can be a great deterrent against sin, and an encouraging prod to a Christ-honoring life.[10]

Suit up daily for the battle. No soldier would go into conflict without his gear. Neither should you. *"Put on the whole armor of God, that you may be able to stand against the wiles of the devil."*[11]

Take the escape hatch. No temptation to sin — that's right, *no* temptation — is beyond the victory Jesus Christ has purchased for you on the Cross. Stand in Christ's victory.[12] Through the Cross, God has disarmed demons and evil authorities,[13] and He has provided a way to escape from every temptation.[14] Take it!

Don't give place to anger. People today are seething with anger. Life will see to it that injustices come your way. When you are wronged, remember that people are not your enemy; they are victims of the enemy. Our enemy is the devil. You cannot allow yourself to stay angry because *"anger gives a foothold to the devil."*[15]

War with an opposite spirit from the prevailing spirit around you. A great weapon against demonic opposition is to counterattack by operating with the opposite spirit. For instance, a spirit of greed is counterattacked by generosity and over-the-top giving. If pride is part of your company's "culture," counter by operating in a spirit of humility. Duplicity is attacked by living with integrity.

Establish a prayer team. More and more businesses owned by Christians are actually employing intercessors. This is an option that should be prayerfully considered. In any event, you can call together a group of people who will consistently pray for you and your calling as Christ's ambassador in the marketplace.[16]

Know your authority in Christ. We can overcome Satan by declarations of God's Word, by understanding the efficacy of the blood of Christ, and by risking for God.[17] You are a God-called businessperson. Effective businesspersons *thrive* in a climate of adversity. You don't have to acquiesce to the enemy. You don't have to surrender to the devil's dominance and somehow convince yourself that it "just must be God's will." This is a fight you can win, and you are destined to win! As someone has said, "You're not going to break, you're going to break records."

Jesus is victor. *"The God of peace will crush Satan under your feet shortly."*[18]

DAY_____DATE_____

DAILY PLANNER

Remember: *"The thief does not come except to steal, and to kill, and to destroy. I have come that they may have life, and that they may have it more abundantly"* (John 10:10).

Reflect: "If we would endeavor, like men of courage, to stand in the battle, surely we would feel the favorable assistance of God from heaven. For He who giveth us occasion to fight, to the end we may get the victory, is ready to succor those that fight manfully, and do trust in His grace." — Thomas à Kempis[19]

Pray: For grace to overcome every attack of the devil against you and your influence in the marketplace for Jesus Christ.

Act: Nullify as of today any *détente* with the devil. How and where do you relax? Have you excused any dishonoring behavior because of your "midlife crisis"? Own up to your spiritual condition and recalibrate for Christ, His Commission, and His Kingdom.

26

The ultimate Partnership

*W*ould you rather be an *employee* or a *partner*? Which of these positions would excite, energize, and motivate you more? I know which I would choose. Most people would prefer to have a piece of the action in steering the future. God put in each of us the drive to excel, achieve, and taste the sweet rewards of accomplishment. He also gave us a deep desire to create and make a significant contribution to something bigger than ourselves. Sadly, many people never experience the satisfaction of this type of work.

But they can. God wants us involved in the biggest, most challenging, and most rewarding project ever given to mankind. This project is called the Great Commission.

In *Doing Business God's Way*, Dennis Peacocke contends that God owns a proprietorship called "Almighty & Sons."[1] He's our boss, and we are proprietors with an ownership stake in His global operations. His business is establishing His ways and His Kingdom on the earth. What a great perspective on life and eternity!

When we were so graciously saved through faith in Christ,[2] our journey of life and purpose really began. Far too many believers look only to the single event of salvation as the end-all. Make no mistake, salvation and rebirth is the greatest gift and miracle. But this new birth is meant to lead us into the most dynamic, exciting, purpose-filled existence there is! Salvation is to be the starting point of partnering with God in the unfolding of His

Kingdom. What a thrilling opportunity and honor! The fact that Almighty God would choose us to co-labor with Him on the earth is astounding. God wants us to be His partners, bringing hope, healing, justice, righteousness, salvation, deliverance, and solutions to our communities and nations. That's why God's people in the business arena are so strategic for fulfilling His purposes. What better platform than the marketplace for the glory of God to shine? What better place than the business arena to influence and reach the lost?

Since God owns the earth and everything in it,[3] His partners should be in the leadership mix of economics, commerce, the arts, and government. That was our Lord's intent when He called us to *"invest this for me while I am gone."*[4] The clear inference in the original language is, "Go into business and make it bigger. Go into government and make it better."

Shouldn't His partners be the ones with the best ideas, the best quality and service, the best work ethic, and the best attitudes? The systems and cycle of sin have dominated the earth and its circles of influence. But as God's people truly wake up to their calling to partnership, His Kingdom manifests in the here and now. Jesus said that the spiritual harvest is plentiful but the workers are few.[5] The harvest field of souls and opportunities is ripe.[6] If Jesus were standing in Wall Street today, I believe He would say the same thing in a different way — *"The harvest is plentiful, but my business partners are few."* Jesus, by the working of the Holy Spirit, is in fact hovering over all the earth, including Wall Street, beckoning us to join Him in His work.

But where are His partners? What have we been doing? Too many have been asleep on the job. They have yet to receive a revelation of their Kingdom job description. Christian businesspersons attend church, hand out bulletins, occasionally volunteer to hang sheetrock, sometimes write a check, don't usually cheat on their taxes, and try to get through this "evil world" without making too many waves. Yawn. The above-mentioned activities are fine, but there is more. Much more! God is looking for genuine business partners. When you begin to look at the world through His lens, your passion, perspective, and purpose comes alive. With this new perspective, our work becomes worship.

Every day we can and should be on mission as an agent of the Most High in the marketplace. Every meeting, project, potential client, and business trip is an opportunity to unpack His splendor. The excellence and quality of our work reflect attitudes toward God and the assignment He has given. Many people will judge us and the God we serve by how they see us work. As business leaders who follow Jesus Christ, our work should be the most diligent, most excellent, and have the most integrity.

There is a clear reason why God brought you into His family — a unique *something* He wants you to accomplish for His sake in your generation. This is your call to "take hold of that for which Christ Jesus took hold of you."[7] Seek God and find out what your unique role is in His plan for the world. There is a contribution to His Kingdom that only you can make. It may be a business, product, or service only you can provide, a song only you can write, a person only you can reach, a new invention you are called to create, a cure you are destined to discover.

It's your unique contribution both to God and humanity. You are God's *"workmanship,"* His *"masterpiece."* You were *"created in Christ Jesus to do good works, which God prepared in advance for us to do."*[8] In other words, God had a specific assignment in mind for you before you were born. He saw a unique contribution for you to make toward the Great Commission and His Kingdom work. Don't sit on the sidelines of life, as so many do. Surrender and join God's Kingdom business as His partner. You're a trusted family partner in "Almighty & Sons."

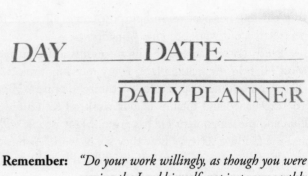

DAY_____DATE_____

DAILY PLANNER

Remember: *"Do your work willingly, as though you were serving the Lord himself, not just your earthly master. In fact, the Lord Jesus is the one you are really serving, and you know that he will reward you"* (Colossians 3:23–24; NLT).

Reflect: "If God is your partner, make your plans big!" — D. L. Moody[9]

Pray: For revelation of God's purposes in all areas of your life.

Act: Do your work today as worship to God.

21

The Weight of Words

Someone once said, "Our words create our worlds." The words we speak shape ours and others' perceptions, perspectives, and cognitive realities. In his book *Church Marketing 101,* Richard Reising contends that marketing is the management of other people's perceptions.[1] Whether you realize it or not, you are constantly "marketing" yourself, your belief systems, and your business to others by the words you say.

If a boss comes into the office and projects negativity by speaking about how terrible things are, how do you think the other employees will react? If that same boss speaks positively and projects confidence, her people will be attracted to follow her leadership. The Bible says the tongue holds the power of life and death.[2] In the business world, when the Chairman of the Fed speaks, his words have the power to dramatically impact financial markets. What we say carries weight that affects our lives and the lives of others.

You've heard the old children's rhyme, *"Sticks and stones may break my bones but words can never hurt me."* Not true! Words go deep into people. You can never take them back. There are 60-year-old men working themselves to death just trying to overcome a hurtful word their father spoke to them when they were kids. Maybe you're one of those people, or you know someone still working through verbal abuse from his or her childhood. Only God can heal wounds caused by words. And He desires for us to bring words of life and healing to others. What we say can literally call forth life or pronounce death. According to Scripture, destructive speech *"can ruin your whole life. It can turn the entire course of your life into a blazing fire of destruction."*[3]

Today you can *speak life to others.* In a world full of bad news and negative reports, an encourager is always a breath of fresh air. The Greek word for encourage is *parakaleo.* A literal meaning of this compound word is to stand beside and to call forth. When we speak positive, affirming words to others, we are calling forth the best in them. We are lifting them to a higher level. People all around us are desperate for affirmation and validation. Anyone who affirms and encourages others regularly will have numerous opportunities to be used by God in a powerful way.

You can have an awesome ministry today — by what you say. *"Let no corrupt word proceed out of your mouth, but what is good for necessary edification, that it may impart grace to the hearers."*[4] You can even *speak life to your circumstances.* How do you speak to your circumstances? You address circumstances through your verbal language, your body language, and your overall mentality toward the situation. Are you viewing problems through your own eyes or through God's eyes? When the option was facing giants or cowering back from victory, it was words that made the difference. One group said, "We're like grasshoppers compared to those giants." But a God-honoring minority said, "These guys are like bread for us to eat. The Lord is with us. Don't be afraid of them."[5] What a difference in perspective.

If you ask God to help you see things the way He sees them, you will view life in an entirely different light. Jesus taught that with just little faith we can speak to our mountains of difficulty and they will move.[6] When faced with difficulties, carry on with confidence, knowing that God is with you and working through the situation for your ultimate good. Scripture is abundantly laced with promises we can claim when we face difficulties.

What are you speaking to your circumstances? Jesus promised dramatic change when a person *"believes that those things he says will be done, he will have whatever he says."*[7]

Today you can *speak life to your inner person.* All of us carry on a constant inner conversation. The thoughts we think and the things we tell ourselves are either confirming what God says about us or aligning with our enemy. Remember, one of the devil's titles is "accuser of the brethren."[8] When we're in an accusative mode — against other believers or even ourselves — we are aligning with Satan's schemes. Let's take a cue from David. He gave his own soul "pep talks" throughout the Psalms. Here's one of them: *"Why are you downcast, O my soul? Why so disturbed within me? Put your hope in God, for I will yet praise him, my Savior and my God."*[9]

What conversations are you having on the inside? Are you speaking God's Word and meditating on it?[10] Are you communing with the Holy Spirit?[11] Your inner thoughts and language will be projected outwardly to others. That's why a job interview can be won or lost in the first 30 seconds, based on the outward portrayal of the inner person. Your words carry weight. Use your words to bring life.

DAY_____DATE_____

DAILY PLANNER

Remember: *The tongue has the power of life and death* (Proverbs 18:21; NIV).

Reflect: "We create with God when we speak the words that God has given us to declare by faith." — Loren Cunningham[12]

Pray: For God to help you speak words of life to yourself, to others, and to your circumstances.

Act: Deal with any hurts caused by others through their words and seek forgiveness if you've wounded another through your words.

28

The Worth of Your Word

*D*o you want to set yourself apart and build a great reputation? Then follow through on your word. I'm not sure there is anything more damaging to our witness and credibility than saying we will do something and then not delivering. Sadly, this is almost the norm in today's world. I can't tell you how many people have told me they'll do this or that, then never followed through. Especially Christians. It often seems as if we're the worst offenders.

When it comes to developing strong relationships, a solid reputation, and a great name in business, nothing comes close to just doing what you say you will do. If you put the fish logo on your business card or advertisement, and claim to be a "Christian-run business," then you had better do what you say. If you state that your service is excellent and you pay on time, then do it! Jesus taught, *"Men will have to give account on the day of judgment for every careless word they have spoken. For by your words you will be acquitted, and by your words you will be condemned."*[1] By being someone who consistently does what you say you will do, you will set yourself apart from everyone else. People will want to do business with you. You will be respected and build a good name.

According to Scripture, a good name is more desirable than great riches.[2] How do you develop a good name? One way is prove that your word can be trusted. Picture each person you come in contact with having a personal bank account where the currency is trust. Each time you make a deal or a promise and deliver the goods, you have deposited trust into their account. You have built rapport and earned a little more trust with that person every time you do what you say.

The opposite is also true. If you say you will do something and you don't, you have made a withdrawal and, consequently, there is a little less "trust" in you in their account. Your word has become less valuable. I have a Christian friend who is a real estate agent. Over a several-year period I've noticed a trend of unmet promises. Most of them are casual things — not returning calls, canceling a lunch at the last minute, forgetting to show up at an agreed-upon meeting, or telling me of projects he's involved with that end up always falling through. I love this brother and still consider him a friend, but do you think I'll use him the next time I'm looking for a real estate agent? No way! He has depleted his trust account over time. It will take quite a while for him to regain my confidence in the legitimacy of his statements.

How refreshing it is when men and women live up to their word! One of the biggest accusations against Christians is that we are hypocrites. Our words and actions aren't consistent. No one is perfect. We're all growing, but we can all make conscious efforts through the enablement of the Holy Spirit to let our words and actions come into alignment. We must remember that people are always observing our lives, our words, and our actions. As someone observed, "You are the only 'Bible' some people will read."

One of the highest virtues in the ancient Roman world was *veritas* — truthfulness. This Latin word today also carries the meaning of weightiness. The words of a truthful person carry weight. The Holy Spirit is referred to as *"the Spirit of truth."*[3] If you can comfortably traffic in untruths, then frankly, you are in very serious trouble. When a believer willfully goes against the truth, he is resisting and grieving the very nature of God's Spirit. King David tried to live a lie until he was confronted by the prophet Nathan.[4] David quickly acknowledged his sin. No more cover-up. In his heart-wrenching prayer of repentance, he acknowledged that God wants our lives to be deeply anchored in truth.[5]

Our word should be trusted. We should be able to stand by our word. *"Let your 'Yes' be 'Yes,' and your 'No,' 'No.' "*[6] This is simply a New Testament reaffirming of the ninth Commandment, *"You shall not bear false witness."*[7] As Christ-followers, we should be distinguished by clear, direct speech. If we will just tell the truth and consistently follow through with verbal commitments, over time our reputation and respect from others will be off the charts. If you have a good name and your word is worth something, prosperity should be a natural by-product. People always prefer to work with someone who is upright, pleasant, fair, and trustworthy. Let your words be worth something.

DAY_____DATE_____

DAILY PLANNER

Remember: *"Let your conversation be always full of grace, seasoned with salt, so that you may know how to answer everyone"* (Colossians 4:6; NIV).

Reflect: Are you a person of your word? Would other people say you are?

Pray: For God to help you follow through with your promises and to practice wisdom before making promises.

Act: Check the promises you have made, then follow through on what you say.

29
Thriving under Threat

ormer chairman of the Federal Reserve Board Alan Greenspan contends that business activity in our day is executed in an "age of turbulence."[1] Best-selling business management writer Tom Peters asserts that "chaos" is the new norm of business and that it is possible to thrive, even in a chaotic climate.[2] But how can you live successfully in a world full of "wars and rumors of wars"?[3]

The apostle Paul showed us the secrets to thriving under threat in his final goodbye to the elders at the church at Ephesus. He was headed for Jerusalem. Paul had been warned prophetically that he would be thrown in jail upon his arrival. In his own words, he knew that *"chains and tribulation"* were just ahead.

With focus and composure Paul said, *"None of these things move me; nor do I count my life dear to myself, so that I may finish my race with joy, and the ministry which I received from the Lord Jesus, to testify to the gospel of the grace of God."*[4] In that single statement, Paul gave us six keys to thriving when threatened.

The first key to thriving under threat is an *unshakable call*. Paul said, *"None of these things move me."* He refused to be intimidated by the threats of prison and even potential martyrdom. When you know who you are in Christ and what He has called you to do, you can face any threat with confidence.

The second key is an *unselfish life*. He said, *"I do not count my life dear to myself."* Paul did not say his life was not valuable; he said his life was not dear *to himself*. He lived from the vantage of being crucified with Christ.[5] The safest place in the world is in the will of God. Jesus taught that in His Kingdom, those who would be self-protective are actually the most at risk. He said, *"If you try to hang on to your life, you will lose it. But if you give up your life for my sake and for the sake of the Good News, you will save it."*[6]

Third, you can thrive under threat if you have an *unstoppable resolve*. Paul was determined to *"finish [his] race with joy."*[7] And he succeeded. Near the end of his life, Paul reported to his faithful friend Timothy that he had completed the life assignment God had given him.[8]

If ever a man had an excuse to quit it was William Carey, the pioneer missionary to India. In 1812, after ten years of painstaking work, Carey watched as a whole decade of his work literally went up in smoke in a suspicious fire. The fire was probably set intentionally by people who were not sympathetic to the message William Carey preached. Can you imagine what went through Carey's heart as he watched his priceless manuscripts — a massive dictionary, two grammar books, and two completed versions of the Bible — go up in flames? (And remember, Carey had no "back-up disk"!) Yet William Carey would literally rise from the ashes. By the end of his life, his accomplishments were staggering, including translating large portions of the Scriptures into an astounding 37 languages and dialects. Carey had an unstoppable resolve.

Fourth, Paul possessed an *irrepressible joy*. Joy becomes even more important *especially* when we are threatened. Paul wrote to the Philippians, *"Rejoice in the Lord. . . . It is a safeguard for you."*[9] This well-grounded joy runs much deeper than shallow happiness or unfounded optimism. This deep, inner joy is the fruit of God's Spirit.[10]

The fifth key for Paul to thriving under threat was an *unearned anointing*. He spoke of a ministry he had *"received from the Lord Jesus."* Paul did not attempt an *achieved* ministry, trying to press into an anointing he did not possess. Rather, he knew that his *received* ministry was as much a gift of grace as salvation itself. It was not earned or deserved. You too have a received ministry — God's calling to represent His Kingdom in the marketplace. As you exercise the gifts God has given you, rather than attempting to minister in areas where you are not gifted, you will experience great joy and fulfillment.

Finally, you can thrive under threat if, like Paul, you have an *undistorted focus*. Paul's life mission statement was a single sentence: *"To testify to the gospel of the grace of God."* You too are called upon to share the good news and extend the fame of Jesus to the ends of the earth.

Trouble and destiny often go hand in hand. Mordecai warned his niece not to hide in her pampered lifestyle and avoid identifying with her people's sufferings. He reminded Queen Esther that playing it safe isn't safe. Like Esther, you have come to the Kingdom for such a time as this.[11] You have been favorably positioned by God with assets and influence you can utilize for Kingdom purposes.

Based on the principles that backed up Paul's resolve, here are some specific steps you can take to thrive when you are under threat:

- Don't try to hide from trouble or from your destiny.
- Take holy risks.
- Determine to finish well.
- Commit to joy.
- Cultivate your "received" ministry.
- Keep your calling in clear view.

DAY_____DATE_____

DAILY PLANNER

Remember: *"Yet who knows whether you have come to the kingdom for such a time as this"* (Esther 4:14).

Reflect: "The achieved ministry will ultimately fail even if, for a period of time, it appears to succeed. The received ministry will ultimately succeed even if, for a period of time, it appears to fail." — Jack Taylor[12]

Pray: That you will finish well and keep your calling in clear view.

Act: Do something today to steward and activate the ministry you have received from the Lord.

30

Dealing with Disaster

*I*t seemed like a regular day at the beach. When the blasts of billions of tons of water wrecked the coasts of 12 Asian nations, most of the people on the beaches were totally unaware of looming tragedy. In its wake, this massive tsunami claimed at least 140,000 lives and left millions homeless. It was one of the largest natural disasters in history.

Life can be like that. The world seems increasingly unstable. We all face constant threats of disruption in forms of terror, dramatic swings in the stock market, currency valuations, and an increased global ripple effect on our economy. The world can be a scary place! Thank God, we have a solid anchor to rely on in times of unpredictability.

Suddenly, without warning, you're hit with a torrent of trouble. How can you survive — and even thrive — in life's sudden tsunamis? Let's look at how we should view life's large-scale disasters. Then let's see how to survive floodtides of trouble that sometimes invade our lives without warning.

Calamities prompt us to ask, "Why?" There are no pat answers. A complete answer will come in heaven when all our questions will be fully resolved by our Father who loves us. Until then we may not be able to understand why such tragedies occur, but it's important that we anchor our attitudes in Scripture. Here are heart attitudes we should maintain.

Show compassion. Christians need to be the first responders in any crisis. God's heart is for people. Every human being should feel a natural humanitarian impulse to help. But compassion is compounded in us as believers because *"the love of God is shed abroad in our hearts by the Holy Ghost."*[1] The Bible calls us to identify with those who suffer. We are to *"weep with those who weep."*[2] Christians should lead the world in responding to human need — and we do. It is a dazzling testimony when Christians rush to meet the needs of all who suffer, no matter what their faith. At the same time, other religions are often sluggish in aiding their own adherents, if they respond at all. Our love speaks volumes. Jesus said, *"Let your light so shine before men, that they may see your good works and glorify your Father in heaven."*[3]

Be slow to judge. In the wake of the Asian tsunami, I heard some Christians say this was God's judgment on non-Christian nations. That is for God to determine, not us. It is true that many of the hardest-hit nations in this tsunami have been some of the most vicious in their persecution of Christians. Still, we need to remember that many Christians lost their lives in this disaster as well. We seem to need a place to pin the blame for tragedies we cannot understand. This was the case when the disciples saw a blind man and immediately assumed his condition was because of someone's sin. *"Who sinned,"* they asked Jesus, *"this man or his parents, that he was born blind?"* Jesus replied that the man's blindness was not because of the man's sin or that of his parents.[4] It is humanity's great thief, the devil, who comes *"to steal, kill and destroy."*[5]

Christians should lead the world in responding to human need — and we do. Our love speaks volumes.

Be quick to repent. Too often we cast aspersions on others without examining our own hearts. It was a common belief in Jesus' day that the men who suffered sudden death when a tower fell on them were worse sinners than others. Jesus rejected such twisted reasoning. *"Do you think they were worse sinners than all other men who dwelt in Jerusalem? I tell you, no; but unless you repent* *you will all likewise perish.*"[6] These are tough words from our Lord. But they call us to examine our own hearts before we judge the spiritual condition of others.

Remember that the earth is under the curse of sin. Not only did man fall with Adam's sin, but the earth itself was affected. The Bible says that the world *"groans and labors with birth pangs."*[7] The result is the actual shifting of the earth that produces natural disasters. The fact is, our planet is not yet fully restored. We look toward Christ's coming rule when there will be *"new heavens and a new earth."*[8]

See natural disasters as a "wake-up call." Jesus promised there would be an increase in natural convulsions just prior to His return. These phenomena would include *"earthquakes in many parts of the world."*[9] Life's sudden tsunamis call us to *"prepare to meet your God."*[10]

DAY_____DATE_____

DAILY PLANNER

Remember: *"Do not be afraid of sudden terror . . . for the Lord will be your confidence, and will keep your foot from being caught"* (Proverbs 3:25–26).

Reflect: "Everything is safe which we commit to Him, and nothing is really safe which is not so committed." — A.W. Tozer[11]

Pray: That you will model stability in a volatile world by your trust in God.

Act: Christians are usually the "first responders" to disasters around the world. What can you do to show God's love when disasters strike?

31

Our Work as Worship

There are two tragic, unbiblical extremes regarding work afoot in our day. The first is laziness. There will always be those who cut corners, those who hope to push the envelope and keep their jobs with minimum effort. Frankly, such persons who claim to be Christians are an embarrassment to the cause of Christ.

Sloth is an archaic word we don't hear used anymore, but it remains a sad reality in the 21st century. It simply means an aversion to work or exertion. You see it everywhere — people who are just couch potato-ing their way through life. This is such a serious affront to God that the old divines placed sloth as one of the Seven Deadly Sins. The dangers of sloth are not just spiritual: *"Lazy hands make a man poor, but diligent hands bring wealth."*[1]

Our work is meant to be a form of worship. In the Benedictine order, work is seen as a spiritual discipline, having equal standing with prayer and study. Ultimately, we are working for God and His glory. *"Whatever you do, work at it with all your heart, as working for the Lord, not for men."*[2] But there's another extreme at the opposite end of the spectrum. It is the equal tragedy of the workaholic. You see them everywhere — people who are securing financially the very families they are losing through overwork. Often these workaholics are running from their families, running from themselves, running from God — or all of the above. Most of all, they're just running.

God instituted a rhythm for work and rest when He commanded, *"Six days you shall labor and do all your work, but the seventh day is the Sabbath of the Lord your God. In it you shall do no work."*[3]

Work is not part of the Curse or a result of the Fall of man. Drudgery associated with work *is* the result of the Fall, but work itself was ordained by God before sin entered into the world. God Himself is a worker — and His greatest masterpiece is human beings.[4] Jesus said He was compelled to do the works of His Father.[5] In His high priestly prayer, He declared He had indeed finished the work given Him by His Father.[6] When Jesus taught the disciples about the great spiritual harvest, He said to pray for more workers — not observers, not critics, *workers.*[7]

Since all of life is to be lived for God's glory, our work should be done:

- *With excellence.* God's work of creation and salvation is excellent in every sense. We glorify Him and acknowledge that we are made in His image when we do our work with excellence.

- *With focus.* The merits of multitasking are overrated. The second century Church father Irenaeus noted, "The glory of God is man fully awake." God is glorified when we are fully awake and focused on the task at hand.

- *By the power of the Holy Spirit.* Through His gifts, fruit, and power, the Holy Spirit gives a "competitive advantage" to believers who want to honor Christ in the workplace. There can be, and should be, a supernatural touch on your life and work.

- *With the right motives.* Don't seek recognition or the applause of people. Rather, seek the applause of heaven. Jesus promised that even small acts of kindness, when done in His name and for His honor, will be openly rewarded.[8]

- *With gratitude.* For the follower of Christ, work is not a grind, it is a gift. Be thankful for the health to work and that people want your goods or services. *"Whatever you do in word or deed, do all in the name of the Lord Jesus, giving thanks to God the Father through Him."*[9]

- *For the glory of God and the extending of His Kingdom.* Your work *is* your ministry. All ministry is to be done *"with the ability which God supplies, that in all things God may be glorified through Jesus Christ."*[10]

- *With a view toward eternity.* Your works will live much longer than you will. At death, Christians *"rest from their labors, and their works follow them."*[11] The Bible indicates we will carry our talents and work acumen into eternity. Our personalities and ethnicities remain in heaven, so why not our abilities? There are eternal uses for our talent we can only imagine. You are practicing for eternity when you practice your gifts and abilities. So today, do your work with all your heart, as unto the Lord.

Oswald Chambers was right: "My life as a worker is the way I say 'thank you' to God for His unspeakable salvation."[12]

DAY_____DATE_____

DAILY PLANNER

Remember: *"For we are His workmanship, created in Christ Jesus for good works, which God prepared beforehand that we should walk in them"* (Ephesians 2:10).

Reflect: "The essence of our work as humans must be that it is done in conscious reliance on God's power, and in conscious quest of God's pattern of excellence, and in deliberate aim to reflect God's glory." — John Piper[13]

Pray: That you will glorify God and advance His Kingdom in and through your work.

Act: Consciously do your work today as unto the Lord and for His glory.

32

Your Competitive Advantage

Many business schools and business books talk about the importance of having a competitive advantage. A competitive advantage exists when there is some superior value or distinction that draws people to a product or service.

Do you realize that, in a real sense, those of us who are in Christ have been given a competitive advantage in life? In Christ, we have been given access and privilege to an element of abundant life that can only be available to those who know Him.[1] This competitive advantage can be harnessed and used to bring honor and glory to God in every aspect of our lives, including business.

We have access to *divine favor*. God's eyes are constantly scanning the earth, looking for hearts who are fully His, so that He might strongly support them.[2] What would it look like if God strongly supported your business efforts?

The closer we draw to God, the more His heart penetrates our hearts. Things begin to come into alignment. Our priorities, plans, and motives all begin to line up with His as we spend time in His presence. Favor may be the most necessary element for promotion, advancement, and acceleration in business. We can boldly ask God for favor, just as Jabez did,[3] provided that our hearts are truly drawn toward Him.

David was confident of God's favor for those in fellowship with Him: *"For You, O Lord, will bless the righteous, with favor You will surround him as with a shield."*[4] Picture your life being "shielded" with God's favor! In business, a shield of favor will land you accounts that you could not have gotten on your own. A shield of favor will help you win the hearts of key decision-makers for no apparent reason. A shield of favor may also protect you from getting a job you thought would be good, but which would have been disastrous. As our hearts and motives align with His, the shield of favor is available for us.

We also have access to *divine creativity*. In Christ, all things were created, and He is the author of creativity.[5] The more we tap into the life-giving vine of Jesus, the more we can plug into His creativity which permeates every area of life.[6] Business rewards creative ideas and solutions. A friend of mine once described our lives as an empty canvas. God gives us the paint colors and the brush and says, *"Go paint for Me a beautiful picture!"*

We have access to *eternal truth* through the Word of God. Often the latest, trendiest business books are simply retelling ancient truths and principles found in the Bible. The Bible has answers to every business challenge.

My friend Mark is a very wealthy, successful businessman in the oil and gas arena. People in our town who know Mark know two things about him. They know that he's a savvy businessperson, and they know that everywhere he goes, his Bible goes with him. Mark's Bible must have several hundred tabs in it where he's marked, circled, and highlighted various verses. One day he told me about his well-worn Bible. "Each one of these tabs represents a problem I've had to deal with and the answer to that problem." What a resource and guide for life we've been given in the Word of God! God has provided a constant source of illumination and guidance for us through His Word.[7] It should be our number one business book.

We have access to *the fruit of the Spirit*. After Paul lists the fruit of the Spirit, he writes, *"Against such things there is no law."*[8] In other words, when we allow the Holy Spirit to operate in and through us, His fruit is acceptable and welcomed in *any* context or setting. God's Spirit enables us to love when others seethe with anger, to display faith-filled peace when others are wracked with fear, and to stay cool when others — well, lose their cool.

Don't ever underestimate the importance of ***discernment***. The Holy Spirit can guide us through discernment, one of the key elements of successful decision-making. We need His discernment to know whether a deal is real or shaky. We need discernment to know who to work with, and who to stay away from. In all things, the closer we are to God the more we will be able to discern His will.[9]

Our competitive advantage — that which will set us apart — is directly linked to the intimacy of our walk with the Lord. The more we draw near to Him and allow His life and Spirit to control us, the more our lives will bear a distinction the rest of the world longs for.

Having access to these privileges does not exclude us from problems or hardships. There is no magic wand we can wave to make all our problems disappear, no magic bullet that will bring instant success. But there is a deeper reservoir of grace, enablement, and anointing we can experience as we press into God.[10] As we mature as persons walking in His presence, we'll become increasingly perceptive to divine ideas, divine opportunities, divine discernment, and divine appointments.

DAY_____DATE_____

DAILY PLANNER

Remember: *"For the eyes of the Lord range throughout the earth to strengthen those whose hearts are fully committed to him"* (2 Chronicles 16:9; NIV).

Reflect: What would it look like if God strongly supported your business efforts? Picture your life being shielded with God's favor.

Pray: For a deeper relationship with God who is the source of favor, creativity, discernment, and fruitful living.

Act: As you seek God, expect His favor and Spirit to reside through you and your business.

33

Your Marketplace Mission

What is your mission? Think about it. Why did God put you *here*, and why did He put you here *now*? God is moving in the marketplace and wants to use businesspersons in a powerful way. The marketplace is where business, government, and education intersect and interrelate. Economics is the fuel behind every major aspect of every culture and society in the world. Sports, entertainment, education, family units, churches and ministries, politics, government, and the arts — they are all affected by economics.

Our God is very strategic. He wants to get His business partners in places of influence in every sector of the marketplace. The marketplace is a ripe mission field where real people interact and grapple with real issues. Business is the vehicle that drives the marketplace. Therefore, godly businessmen and women who possess a Kingdom vision and mission are strategic in His plan for the world.

Jesus commissioned the Church to be about the business of preaching the gospel and making disciples in every nation.[1] From the beginning, God directed man to take dominion and steward the earth.[2] For God's people to be effective in these two primary tasks, we must make Jesus center stage. The Church's greatest strength is not when it is gathered but when it is scattered as salt and light throughout the marketplace. Jesus said we are the salt — not of the Church but *"of the earth."*[3] Salt adds flavor, preserves from corruption, and sometimes stings as it heals. We are called by our Lord to do the same. Jesus said we are the light — again, not of the

Church but *"of the world."*[4] Light dispels darkness, brings warmth, and uncovers what is hidden. Our lives are to do the same.

Tragically, Christians today are often known more for what we are *against* than what we are *for*. Yet we are called not so much to criticize culture as we are called to create it. It seems that much of the time Christians like to hide inside our churches and talk about how bad it is "out there in the world." Yet if our culture is crumbling, it is because our salt has not been potent and our light has been dim. We will never fulfill the Great Commission until our local churches truly become equipping centers for sending the saints into their ministry assignment — outside the walls of the church!

Look at the effects of globalization. Nations are more inter-related than ever in history, and business is the driving force. A new army of Kingdom-minded businesspersons must be raised up to bring Jesus into the marketplaces of every nation. Some nations may be closed to traditional missionaries, but almost every nation flings its doors wide open to international businesses.

Jesus in the marketplace takes many forms, resulting in the transformation of lives and culture. When the gospel of the King-dom is preached, there is a natural lifting of values, dignity, and collective worth, and respect for individuals and communities. Here is a glimpse of how Jesus is operating in the marketplace:

- New businesses are started that have more than just a profit motivation. They go beyond the bottom line. These King-dom businesses create fair-paying jobs. They are generous with profits and bring economic and spiritual blessings to their communities and the world.

- New capital is generated by believers in businesses that will bless the Church and God's Kingdom purposes. Em-ployees, vendors, customers, and even competitors will see Christ at work through His people.

- People are saved, healed, and delivered from all kinds of garbage because of the influence and testimony of Spirit-filled co-workers.

- Kingdom businesspersons are known by the quality and standards of the products and services they produce. Their business transactions are carried out with integrity.

- Corruption declines and biblical standards of honesty and trust create a healthy business climate.

When Jesus is Lord in the marketplace, prosperity is the result. Ask yourself, *"Where do I fit* and *where does Jesus fit* in my work and influence in the marketplace?" In the past, you may have separated your professional life and church life. Perhaps God is stirring your heart and challenging you to think in new paradigms. He longs to permeate all aspects of your life, and He wants to use you as His agent for change in the marketplace. God is all about total integration. Jesus is Lord, not only in our families and local churches — He is also Lord of business, education, government, entertainment, media, and the arts. Submit to His Lordship today and invite His manifest presence into your life work.

DAY_____DATE_____

DAILY PLANNER

Remember: *"Fill the earth and subdue it; have dominion . . ."* (Genesis 1:28).

Reflect: "There is not a square inch in the whole of human existence over which Christ, who is sovereign over all, does not cry, 'Mine!'" — Abraham Kuyper[5]

Pray: For a clear mission regarding your role in the marketplace. Pray for God's Spirit to sweep across the business arenas of the world.

Act: Carry the mindset of being Christ's ambassador[6] in every jurisdiction of life.

Part III

LEAVING A LEGACY

For Christ, His Commission, and His Kingdom

34

A Multigenerational Mindset

Edmund Burke said, "History is a pact between the dead, the living, and the yet unborn."[1]

What's your vision? What drives you? What kind of dreams and goals do you have for your life? I would like to submit this thought: God's vision and dreams for your life are to impact generations after you are gone. In other words, if your vision does not exceed your lifetime, it is too short and too shallow.

God would have us answer this daunting question: *What am I doing to impact the next generation?* This can apply to our physical sons and daughters, our spiritual children, and those we are mentoring in business.

Most of the great cathedrals in Europe were built over the span of several generations. It was not uncommon for the first planning generation of builders to plant trees that would someday provide wood for the beams. This wood would be used by the original planters' grandchildren. That's a beautiful picture of God's multigenerational purpose for our lives. We're to have an impact and a role in shaping the future.

Think of the many times Scripture refers to God as *"the God of Abraham, Isaac, and Jacob."* God's view is omnidirectional. He is already planning what He will do in future generations through the choices we make now.

God has taken you on as a lifetime project — and He has gone on sworn record that He will complete what He has started in you.[2] Many of us read Philippians 1:6 and assume it means God will finish the good things in us until the day we die. But that's not what the verse says. *"The day of Christ Jesus"* refers to the future time when Christ returns and sets up His unrivaled rule over the earth. That means the good things He is working in and through us will have bearing on generations to come after we are gone.

Sadly, many people stay stuck in the same debilitating cycles that entrapped their predecessors. They repeat the same mistakes and fall for the same traps as their parents and grandparents. But our past *never* has to determine our future. Even if you are a first-generation Christian, you are a brand new creation in Christ. The destructive patterns of your family's past have been dealt with at the Cross. The legacy of your family's future can start with *you*.[3]

In my book, *Living as if Heaven Matters,* I wrote, "One hundred years from today your present income will be inconsequential. . . . Whether you threw pizza dough for a living, threw strikeouts for a major league team, or threw your weight around in some corporate boardroom as a CEO just won't matter. It will matter that you knew God. It will greatly matter . . . that you made a commitment of your life to Jesus Christ. . . . It will matter that you fit into God's purposes for your life and for your time."[4]

Single generational thinking stifles everything from economic prosperity to spiritual strength. The devil loves the weapon of short-term living. God's plan, on the other hand, is for each generation to build upon the good of previous eras. Head starts are always better than dead starts.

An interesting phenomenon happens in relay races. Have you noticed that the next runner takes the baton at the point of full acceleration? When it's time for your children, those you mentor, your apprentices and protégés to receive their "baton," will they be starting with the blessings of full momentum, or will they take the baton from a dead start?

This transgenerational principle applies to all arenas of life, including business. What do you want your business to look like ten years from now? Twenty years? Fifty years? What about your employees and staff? The things you are doing today in your business operations are affecting the future outcome of the company.

The way you interact with those you work with has bearing on the imprint you're making in their lives. Our job as mentors, managers, and leaders should be to bring out the best of what God has put in those we help lead.

There is an old saying, "There is no success without a successor." You should be in the process of training and molding future proprietors to either take your place or help run the business in your absence. Who is your successor?

The apostle Paul understood this principle well. He was constantly pouring his life into others, notably a young pastor named Timothy. And he charged him to continue the process of equipping others.[5] When writing to the Philippians, Paul admonished them to continue their good works, even much more in his absence.[6] Paul understood that while he was present with the believers, they would know he was watching and be apt to behave correctly. But the time came for them to grow and act maturely on their own, outside of his presence. The truths Paul had downloaded in them were now to be lived out though their mentor was no longer with them.

The business or company you are in today may not be around 50 years from now. But the intangible assets and the eternal wealth of your character, values, skills, and good works can live on and affect generations to come, long after you're gone.

Live in such a way that your life will make a lasting imprint on future generations.

DAY_____DATE_____

DAILY PLANNER

Remember: *"And the things that you have heard from me among many witnesses, commit these to faithful men who will be able to teach others also"* (2 Timothy 2:2).

Reflect: "Measure your success in light of this question: What am I doing to impact the next generation for Jesus Christ?" — Howard Hendricks[7]

Pray: For God to show you how to think and act multigenerationally, and to implement a multi-generation strategy.

Act: Write your multigenerational vision for your personal life, your family, and your marketplace ministry.

35

Bottom-line Passion

"Man, what's *driving* you anyway?" A well-meaning friend was probing me, asking me to explain to him just why I go to several of the world's hot spots and voluntarily leave the comforts of home. My friend asked me again, "David, what's driving you?"

It's a good question. And here's the short answer: *I long to see Jesus known, loved, and worshiped by every tribe, language, and nation.* I *crave* to see Him honored among all nations. It's my passion and purpose. This passion puts me in very good company. God Himself is passionately committed to the worldwide acclaim of His Son. *"[Christ's] government and its peace will never end. . . . The passionate commitment of the LORD of the Heaven's Armies will make this happen!"*[1]

And, by the way, what's driving *you*?

When our sons were small, Naomi and I would tuck the boys into their beds at night and sing to them. But it was no lullaby! As our boys drifted off to sleep, we would sing,

> *Rise up, O men of God,*
> *Have done with lesser things.*
> *Give heart and soul and mind and strength*
> *To serve the King of kings!*[2]

Let me ask you point-blank: Is your heart still wrapped around "lesser things"? If so, when is it going to end? When will *your* priorities line up with *God's* priorities? *When?*

Missionary Francis Xavier sent word back to the dispassionate students of his day, urging them to passion for God's purposes. He pled with them to "give up their small ambitions and come eastward and preach the gospel of Christ!"[3]

What are your ambitions? How big are they? How worthy are they? What are you giving your life for — and why? After Isaiah's encounter with the glory of God, he immediately heard a missionary call: *"Whom shall I send, and who will go for Us?"* His immediate response was, *"Here am I! Send me."*[4] Today you are being sent into the arena of the marketplace — for Christ and His Kingdom.

When we truly experience God's glory, we will burn with a passion for His glory. With the Psalmist, our hearts will cry out, *"Be exalted, O God, above the heavens; let Your glory be over all the earth!"*[5]

I'm calling you to give up your small ambitions. *To know Him and to make Him known! To love Him and to make Him loved!* Let this be your blazing passion.

It was this drive for God's global glory that thrust the early Christians beyond themselves. *"It was for the sake of the Name that they went out."*[6] They ached for the fame of His name! With the Psalmist, their hearts' desire was, *"May the peoples praise You, O God; may all the peoples praise you."*[7]

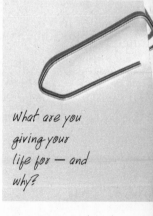

What are you giving your life for — and why?

Those who die without faith in Jesus Christ are eternally lost. Surely that should make us missions activists. But it is not our highest motivation. The needs of humanity are immense and desperate. We should identify with those who suffer and seek to heal the open, festering wounds of our world. Although noble, this humanitarian impulse should not be our highest motivation, either. Talk of "discovering our destiny" is sometimes just thinly veiled egotism. If "fulfilling our purpose" simply means doing all *I* want with *my* life, we're carnal narcissists, no matter how much we may protest to the contrary. But if "fulfilling our purpose" means throwing all our energies, gifts, and influence into extending *His* glory throughout the earth, then we're getting the point.

What would be the greatest offering of gratitude we could give for Christ's sacrifice on the Cross for us? Paul gives us the astounding answer. He said he had *"the priestly duty of proclaiming the gospel of God, so that the nations might become an offering acceptable to God, sanctified by the Holy Spirit."*[8] In other words, the greatest gift of worship we could ever present to God would be to offer redeemed nations that His blood has purchased back to Him! And how does this happen? By transforming nations with the power of the gospel and principles of His Kingdom!

With Paul, our highest motivation should be to offer all peoples to God as trophies of His grace that He might receive the worth and honor that is due only to Him. It's no wonder that the new song of the redeemed from every tribe, language, and people peals out with the loud declaration, *"Worthy is the Lamb who was slain, to receive power and wealth and wisdom and strength and honor and glory and praise!"*[9]

We long for His honor throughout all the earth. It's our bottom-line passion.

> *My gracious Master and my God,*
> *Assist me to proclaim,*
> *To spread through all the earth abroad*
> *The honors of Thy name.*[10]

DAY_____DATE_____

DAILY PLANNER

Remember: *"Go therefore and make disciples of all the nations, baptizing them in the name of the Father and of the Son and of the Holy Spirit, teaching them to observe all things that I have commanded you; and lo, I am with you always, even to the end of the age"* (Matthew 28:19–20).

Reflect: "Our hearts have room only for one all-embracing devotion, and we can cleave to only one Lord." — Deitrich Bonhoeffer[11]

Pray: "God, I pray Thee, light these idle sticks of my life and may I burn for Thee. Consume my life, my God, for it is Thine." (Jim Elliot)[12]

Act: What is your bottom-line passion? What will you do today as a result of that passion?

36
Integrity

A few years ago I was interviewed by a Christian magazine on the subject of changes in ministry in America. The question posed to me was, "How will ministry in America change in the first decade of the 21st century?"

I responded, "Trust will be harder to gain and easier to lose."

The trust factor of the general public toward church and business leaders is at an all-time low — and regrettably, for good reason. A slew of scandals over the last 20 years have jaundiced most people's view of leaders. Credibility has cratered. But God's standard has not been lowered, and there is a fresh call for integrity.

The word *integrity* is derived from a mathematical term — integer. As you probably remember from school, an integer is a whole number; it is not fractioned. In the same way, a person of integrity is a whole person. There is no degree of difference between his or her public persona and the true private person.

A person loses integrity when there is any degree of difference between what people perceive him to be (the public persona) and who he truly is in private (the real person). To whatever degree the private person differs from the public persona, to that degree the person has lost integrity.

D.L. Moody said, "Character is what you are in the dark."[1] And Booker T. Washington observed, "Character is power."[2] How true this is in business, since business relationships are built on the confidence people place in us to deliver on what we say. So, how can you build and buttress personal integrity? Here are steps you can take.

Daily humble yourself before God. Twice in the New Testament we are specifically told to humble ourselves before God.[3] Those who do so don't have to worry about being self-promoting. The Bible promises that God Himself will promote them. Further, He will give His enabling grace to them.[4]

Fred Smith Sr. was a sought-after consultant to many companies and ministries. He observed, "Humility is not denying the power you have. It is realizing that the power comes through you, not from you."[5] Far from being arrogant, the truly great take the low place. And this is exactly the style of servant-leadership Jesus taught. He contrasted His leadership style with the prevailing philosophies of egocentric dominance: *"You know that in this world kings are tyrants, and officials lord it over the people beneath them. But among you it should be quite different. Whoever wants to be a leader among you must be your servant."*[6] No wonder Andrew Murray regarded humility as "the mother virtue and the perpetual safeguard of the soul."[7]

Be accountable. For over a decade I have been in an accountability relationship with a trusted peer in ministry. Every three weeks we meet and hold each other's feet to the fire with very pointed questions regarding daily time with God, the condition of our marriages, what we have viewed, how we have handled money, if we have been with a woman "in an inappropriate way or what others could view as inappropriate," and the use of our time. I'm very grateful for this level of personal accountability.

Early on, Billy Graham and his team committed to mutual accountability. They established internal safeguards concerning honesty, integrity, purity, and humility. The Bible says, *"As iron sharpens iron, so one man sharpens another."*[8]

Get in God's Word. *"How can a young man keep his way pure?"* the Bible asks. The answer: *"By living according to your word."*[9]

Submit to God's discipline. When we are duplicitous, God disciplines us as a loving Father. We should be grateful for the disciplining hand of God; it is a reminder that we are His children and He has committed Himself to our maturity.[10] In fact, He won't quit until we are conformed into the image of Christ.[11]

The end result of God's discipline is *"that we may be partakers of His holiness."*[12] Be grateful for your Heavenly Father's discipline because, as Dale O'Shields reminds us, "God promotes those who pass their tests."[13]

Keep short accounts with God. We can trust God's indwelling Spirit to flag us whenever sin creeps into our lives — whether it comes in the form of unrighteous thoughts, words, or deeds. Whenever the Holy Spirit spotlights any sin, confess and turn from it immediately. The Bible promises, *"If we confess our sins, He is faithful and just to forgive us our sins and to cleanse us from all unrighteousness."*[14] By acknowledging and repenting of any and all sin, and by receiving God's gracious forgiveness, we can live in perpetual fellowship with God.

Every God-honoring action is a deposit in the spiritual and moral capital in the "trust fund" of your nation. And every breakdown of integrity depletes the spiritual and moral capital of your nation.

We need constant vigilance, remembering that it is *"the little foxes that ruin the vineyards."*[15] A single indiscretion can ruin a lifetime of character development. Make no allowance for rebellion, no matter how small it may seem. It's well worth asking — what indulgences are you allowing yourself as some kind of emotional reward for the load you are carrying?

Reflect on the consequences of rebellion and obedience. Spiritual and moral capital. Every God-honoring action is a deposit of spiritual and moral capital in the "trust fund" of your nation. And every breakdown of integrity depletes the spiritual and moral capital of your nation. According to Scripture, a good name is to be prized over riches.[16]

Live in light of the Judgment Seat of Christ. As believers, our entire post-conversion life will come up for review when we stand before the Lord. There will be a very thorough "line item accounting" for all we have done, good or bad.[17] Living *this day* in light of *that day* goes a long way toward ensuring integrity.

DAY_____DATE____

DAILY PLANNER

Remember: *"He who walks in integrity walks securely, but he who perverts his ways will be found out"* (Proverbs 10:9; NASB).

Reflect: "Leadership requires moral authority. Followers will only trust leaders who exhibit the highest level of integrity." — Bill Hybels[18]

Pray: That the Holy Spirit will reveal any duplicity in your life.

Act: Resolve to live in integrity. Check your life for "small allowances" that could, in time, shipwreck your reputation.

31

Your Greatest Asset

Your biggest investment and your greatest asset is your family.

A recent groundbreaking research report by the Center for Relationship Enrichment at John Brown University has quantified the economic impact that can be associated with family fragmentation. The study shows that U.S. taxpayers pay a minimum of $112 billion annually due to costs for anti-poverty, criminal justice, and educational programs and due to reduced taxes paid by individuals whose productivity has been negatively affected by family instability. No matter your current family situation or marital status, the insights and principles you will discover in this chapter are both powerful and relevant.

"We can no longer say that what happens in my neighbor's house is not my business and does not affect me or my family or my community," notes Dr. Gary Oliver, executive director of the center. "When marriages and families suffer, our community suffers."[1]

Several years ago an entrepreneur who was in the middle of a divorce showed me his collection of sports cars. He was clearly proud of them. Each one was polished and impeccably clean. So I asked him, "What would happen if you just let these cars sit and didn't pay attention to them?"

"Man, are you crazy?" he replied. "Pretty soon, if I didn't protect them, they would start to rust — and my investment in these babies is far too important to let that happen." Caught up short, he realized he was stung by his own words. He had given more weight to the corrosion of his cars than the corrosion of his marriage.

God isn't calling you to win the world and in the process lose your marriage. Our priorities should be 1) our relationship with God, 2) our relationship with our spouse and family, and 3) the work He has given us. Why? Because the quality of our work and service is directly linked to the health of our most important relationships. Don't let the demands of life reverse the order.

Today we want to talk especially to husbands. Men, there's no way to spin the clear teaching of Scripture. Your family's spiritual health is your responsibility. It's your biggest investment. And husbands are to show the same sacrificial love for their wives that Jesus shows for us.[2]

Your relationship with your wife is your most precious earthly relationship. God requires husbands to love their wives and to commit themselves to the spiritual growth of their wives.[3] And there are some clear steps you can take every day to strengthen your biggest investment. Studies consistently show that most millionaires have strong marriages. The man who protects his biggest investment will also care for his other investments.

God isn't calling you to win the world and in the process lose your family.

Each day is an opportunity to make your marriage either better or worse. Note well this story from Proverbs: *"I walked by the field of a lazy person, the vineyard of one with no common sense. I saw that it was overgrown with nettles. It was covered with weeds. . . . Then, as I looked and thought about it, I learned this lesson: A little extra sleep, a little more slumber, a little folding of the hands to rest — then poverty will pounce on you like a bandit; scarcity will attack you like an armed robber."*[4] This is a sobering reminder to be diligent both in business and marriage. Men, cultivate the field of your marriage.

These four simple practices will go a long way toward strengthening your marriage:

- Every day, pray together.
- Every day, tell your wife you love her.
- Every day, do something to help her.
- Every day, pay her a sincere compliment.

Now, let's talk about sexual temptations and faithfulness to your marriage vows. Let's get real. Although all sin is to be shunned, sexual sins usually cause more damage than other sins. The results of immorality are far-reaching. Don't buy in to the foolish lie that it's okay, "if nobody gets hurt." Let me ask you: Have you *ever* seen a case of unfaithfulness where nobody got hurt?

Our bodies are the temple of the Holy Spirit.[5] As Christians we are to control our bodies and live in holiness and honor.[6] Right now, let me encourage you to pause and make a fresh presentation of your body and your life to the Lord.[7]

You might be struggling with a love that has grown cold. The Bible shows you how to recover love that has been lost. Although the church at Ephesus was patient and hardworking, they too had lost their first love, their love for Jesus.[8] Here is the prescription He gave them to recover their lost love for Him. These principles apply in any relationship where love has been lost.

- **Remember.** Make your mind work for your marriage, not against it. Remember your wedding vows. Remember the wonderful times you have experienced together. Remember the beauty of your first love.

- **Repent.** Repent of your cold heart toward your wife. Determine to turn around. The Greek meaning for "repent" is "to change the mind." So, change your mind about your marriage. Stop believing the devil's lies. Renew your mind by God's Word. Change your mind and turn away from anything that is unhealthy in your marriage.

- **Do the first works.** What did you do when you were first in love? Do those things again. Did you bring her flowers? Did you frequently tell her you loved her? Were you affectionate toward her? Begin today to do the first works.

You've probably heard the old story of the man admiring the farmer's field. "The Lord sure made a beautiful field of crops," the visitor observed. "Yes sir," the farmer replied, "but you shoulda seen this field when the Lord had it all to Himself!" God stands ready to pour life-giving sunshine and refreshing rain on your biggest investment — your marriage and family — but He expects you to plow the field.

DAY_____DATE_____

DAILY PLANNER

Remember: *"Husbands, love your wives, just as Christ also loved the church and gave Himself for her"* (Ephesians 5:25).

Reflect: "Sustain a family life for a long period of time and you can sustain success for a long period of time. First things first. If your life is in order you can do whatever you want." — Pat Riley[9]

Pray: For your spouse, for your marriage, for grace to cultivate your relationship with your spouse, and for the fruit of the Spirit to be ever increasing in your life.

Act: Commit to start today the four suggested practices that can strengthen your marriage.

38

Your Unique Contribution

God has made you to potentially be the world's best at something. And it is incumbent upon you to discover what that "something" is.

The apostle Paul was determined to lay hold of the specific reason for which Christ had laid hold of him.[1] As Jeff McLoud observes, "Salvation is not just being saved *from* something, it is being saved *for* something."[2]

Has it occurred to you that God loves you so much He wants you to invest your life in what you actually enjoy and are fulfilled in doing? There was an observable restlessness in Winston Churchill's life — until, at age 70, he was called to be prime minister and rescue his nation from its greatest peril. Although it was a season of immense difficulty, Churchill exulted in the challenge. He was literally made for it. Concerning his World War II leadership Churchill recalled, "I felt as if I were walking with destiny, and that all my past life had been but a preparation for this hour and for this trial."[3]

There is destiny over your life, as well. There is a unique contribution you are to make, and all your past life has been preparation for it. God told Jeremiah that His eye had been on him even before he was conceived, and that God had already ordained a holy calling for his life.[4]

There is a calling on your life, as well. "A calling," writes Os Guinness, "is the truth that God calls us to Himself so decisively that everything we are, everything we do, and everything we have, is invested with a special devotion to His summons and service."[5] Your calling is first a call to intimacy and devotion to God. From that place He will call you to your unique "summons and service."

How do you discover your specialized summons, your destiny? How do you find where to make your unique contribution? You must first discover the five components that coalesce to form your unique calling.[6] Those components are:

Anointing. The anointing is the Holy Spirit activated in you in a particular arena of life and ministry. Anointing unleashes the supernatural. When you serve God under His Spirit's anointing, all things are possible. When you minister in the realm of your anointing, there is a certain ease in what you do. Although you may grow tired physically, there is also a built-in rejuvenation even as you work. Anointed work is edifying and fulfilling.

When you're anointed, God's enabling grace is dynamically working. This anointing of the Spirit enables you to fulfill your calling, your life assignment. There is a realm of anointing unique to every believer. As Ed Silvoso wrote, many are literally "anointed for business."[7] That leads us to the second component of the sweet spot.

Gifts. The New Testament describes gifts of the Holy Spirit that are available to you.[8] Certain spiritual gifts are dominant in your life. These dominant gifts are dispensed expressly to equip you for your life calling and your unique contribution. But spiritual gifts can ossify through disuse, or when you rely on past patterns rather than present tense sensitivity to God's Spirit. That is why Paul urged Timothy, *"Stir up the gift of God which is in you."*[9] When spiritual gifts are activated and ministered in the Spirit's anointing, you're finding your unique contribution.

Abilities. Natural abilities are not spiritual gifts, but they almost always complement them. God has blessed you with some natural abilities. In the movie *Chariots of Fire,* Eric Liddell makes a profound statement about natural abilities and finding your unique calling. "God made me for a purpose — for China," Liddell observed in reference to his destiny. "But He also made me fast, and when I run, I feel His pleasure." This is a reference to the smile of God on Liddell's employing of a God-given natural ability. What ability do you have that, when you exercise it, you feel God's pleasure?

Passion. What do all great leaders possess in common? In a word, passion. Passion is the internal fuel that propels you toward your God-ordained destiny. Preceding vision and mission statements or structure, somebody's heart has to be in white-hot upheaval.

What breaks your heart? What makes you weep or makes you want to pound the table? This is a huge clue to your core passion. And your core passion is a huge clue to your distinct destiny.

Need. What do you personally view as an intolerable condition? William Wilberforce, a wealthy businessman and politician, came to see slavery anywhere in the British Empire as simply intolerable. William Carey could not tolerate an unevangelized, illiterate India. Martin Luther could not tolerate a perversion of the gospel, and Martin Luther King Jr. could not tolerate a segregated America.

If you can rest comfortably with a blind eye to the ravaged conditions of our world, then frankly you are way too comfortable. A colossal iniquity is that far too many people are couch-potatoing their way through life with no sense of holy calling and mission. The apostle Paul wrote, *"Necessity is laid upon me."*[10] What is *your* holy imperative? What work does your heart say, *"This* I *must* do"?

Our planet is engulfed in human need — but the whole global tsunami of pain is not your assignment. That would be literally overwhelming. But if you will search your soul, God will trigger your passion. A clear call to throw your life into alleviating a specific need will tug at your heart. It will demand your involvement and intervention. That is your life's unique contribution.

Where the Spirit's anointing, spiritual gifts, natural abilities, dominant passion, and human need connect — this is where you will find your life's calling and make your unique contribution. The more you connect *there,* the greater your impact will be.

DAY_____DATE_____

DAILY PLANNER

Remember: *"Before I shaped you in the womb, I knew all about you. Before you saw the light of day, I had holy plans for you . . ."* (Jeremiah 1:5; MSG).

Reflect: "Whatever you do, find the God-centered, Christ-exalting, Bible-saturated passion of your life, and find your way to say it and live for it and die for it." — John Piper[11]

Pray: That you will fulfill your unique calling and make your unique contribution to God's purposes in your generation.

Act: What will you do today toward making your unique contribution?

39

Leave a Legacy

*W*hat will be your epitaph?

Nikolas von Zinzendorf was a wealthy, titled man. He could have lived a life of ease — and aimlessness. Had he chosen to live only to satisfy himself, his epitaph might well have been:

HERE LIES
NIKOLAS ZINZENDORF
WEALTHY LAND BARON

And that would have been the end of the story. Big deal.

But one day, strolling through an art gallery as a young man, everything changed. Suddenly Zinzendorf was arrested by a powerful depiction of Christ's passion. Zinzendorf stared motionless at the painting, transfixed by the power of its message. This wealthy, young nobleman was deeply moved that afternoon in the art gallery as he viewed the magnificent painting of Jesus being reviled before Pilate with the Latin inscription, *Ecce Homo,* "Behold, the Man."[1]

As Zinzendorf meditated on the sacrifice of Christ for him, the Lord spoke to his heart through that painting, "This I have done for you. What have you done for Me?"

In that European art gallery Zinzendorf's heart was broken and his life refocused. Rejecting the life of ease he had enjoyed as an aristocrat, he gave himself completely to the spread of the gospel. The Cross of Christ had captured his heart.

Years after Zinzendorf's encounter in the art gallery he gave refuge on his estate to the zealous missionary group, the Moravians.

Zinzendorf would later lead a communion service that sparked a missions prayer meeting that went nonstop for the next one hundred years. Many young Moravians launched out from that pivotal meeting as missionaries, some even voluntarily selling themselves into slavery in order to reach unevangelized slaves. Their rallying cry was Zinzendorf's challenge, stemming from that fresh vision of the Cross — "to win for the Lamb the reward of His sacrifice."

Today, Nikolas Zinzendorf is remembered — not because he possessed great wealth, but because of how he stewarded that wealth and leveraged his life for the gospel.

What legacy will you leave? Edmund Burke observed that our lives are intertwined in "a spiritual union of the dead, the living and those yet unborn."[2] We have a responsibility both to the past and the future. What are you doing today that will be of value one hundred years from now? What are you doing today that will last for eternity? Cultivating your most strategic relationships impacts Christ's Kingdom now — and well past your lifetime. Daily deepening your relationship with God, nurturing relationships with your family and close friends, and pouring your life into the next generation of leaders has Kingdom value now and for future generations.

As you finish this book, you should know we have prayed for you and everyone who picks up this book. Our prayer is that you will leave . . .

A legacy of integrity. *Your choices are only two: a memory that is blessed or a tainted legacy.* Don't leave your children the burden of carrying a rotting name. *"The memory of the righteous is blessed, but the name of the wicked will rot."*[3] Your sins also set in motion a destructive cycle that will reach down to your great-grandchildren, unless it is broken by God's grace.[4] Conversely, *"humility and the fear of the Lord bring wealth and honor and life."*[5]

A legacy of faith. On December 31, 1999, we gathered our extended family for a celebration of God's faithfulness to our family throughout the 20th century. We also officially dedicated our family to Christ and His Kingdom purposes for the next one hundred years. We claimed God's promise to bless the righteous and give peace to their children.[6] We encourage you to do the same. If you are a follower of Jesus Christ, there is no reason why you should not expect and believe that all your children, grandchildren, and great-grandchildren will love and follow Him too.

A legacy of faithfulness. I talked to a prominent lawyer whose grandfather was once a well-known preacher. In this man's latter years, he suddenly divorced his wife and promptly married his secretary. "It's 30 years later," the lawyer said, "and our family is just now beginning to recover." May those who come behind us find us faithful — to our spouses, to our calling, and to Christ.

A legacy of fruitfulness. May people be in heaven because you lived. May companies — and even countries — be transformed because you lived. May the Great Commission be much closer to the Great Completion because you lived. Much fruit brings glory to Christ and verifies that we are truly His disciples.[7]

A brief word also needs to be said about the infamous "midlife crisis." This lame concession has become a very handy excuse for all sorts of human train wrecks. Indiscretions you seek to somehow justify by emotional issues in your middle years can forever ruin your legacy. Don't engage in détente with the devil. He aims to *"sift you as wheat."*[8] A good portion of the junk people are trying to "work through" in counseling offices or even in their prayer times is "deals" they've made with the devil.

One of the most serious questions you could ask is, *what "indulgences" am I allowing to compensate for the load I'm carrying?* The key to overcoming a midlife crisis is to calibrate on leaving a legacy for Christ, His Commission, and His Kingdom. As Chuck Swindoll wrote, "When I appreciate that every breath I suck into my lungs is a gift from God, purchased by His Son's agony on the Cross, how can I waste it on self-interest?"[9]

More than anything else, we pray that your life will leave the fragrance of Jesus.[10] And when you stand before Him to give an account of your life, may you hear from His lips those words that are more precious than life itself: *"Well done, good and faithful servant."*[11]

At the end, when you transition from time to eternity, may you leave a legacy of genuine success — a life lived beyond the bottom line. The base line that ultimately matters isn't at the end of your ledger; it's at the end of your life.

A truly successful life is measured not by its duration but by its direction; not by its parties but by its purpose; not by what was amassed but by what was dispersed; not by the embracing of things but by embracing the one thing — to love Jesus and to make Him loved by people everywhere.

DAY_____ DATE_____

DAILY PLANNER

Remember: *"Blessed is the man who fears the LORD, who delights greatly in His commandments. His descendants will be mighty on earth; the generation of the upright will be blessed"* (Psalm 112:1–2).

Reflect: "Those who leave a Christ-honoring legacy see the invisible, hear the inaudible, and embrace the imperishable. As a result, they can do with Christ what is impossible without Him. They exit earth strong in spirit, happy and brimming with hope — solid, immovable, biblical hope. What a legacy."[12]

Pray: That you will leave a legacy that will glorify God and bring honor to Jesus Christ.

Act: Write out your epitaph, as you would want to be remembered. Begin today intentionally living so that you will be remembered in that way.

Endnotes

Introduction
1. Marc Gunther, "God & Business," *Fortune* (July 9, 2001): p. 66.
2. Matthew 5:13–14.
3. 2 Corinthians 5:20.

Chapter 1: Giving Living
1. Franklin Graham with Jeanette Lockerbie, *Bob Pierce: This One Thing I Do* (Waco, TX: Word Books, 1983), p. 183.
2. Luke 12:15–21.
3. Luke 12:15.
4. Matthew 6:19–21.
5. Luke 12:48.
6. Robert Morris, *The Blessed Life* (Southlake, TX: Gateway Church, 2002), p. 168.

Chapter 2: Money: Trap or Tool?
1. 1 Timothy 6:10.
2. Philippians 4:19.
3. Matthew 6:31–33.
4. 1 Timothy 6:5.
5. James 2:5.
6. James 1:17; 1 Corinthians 4:7.
7. Proverbs 27:24.
8. Matthew 6:19–21.
9. Rick Warren, *The Purpose Driven Life* (Grand Rapids, MI: Zondervan, 1983), p. 267.

Chapter 3: Money Musings
1. Proverbs 13:22.
2. John 17:3.
3. Genesis 15:1.
4. 1 Timothy 6:5.
5. Colossians 3:1–2.
6. 1 John 3:17.
7. Sherwood Eliot Wirt, Kersten Beckstrom, eds., *Total Encyclopedia of Living Quotations* (Minneapolis, MN: Bethany House, 1974), p. 159.
8. Richard A. Swenson, M.D., *Margin* (Colorado Springs, CO: NavPress, 2004), p. 137.
9. Proverbs 23:5.
10. 1 Timothy 6:17–18.

11. Robert Morris, *The Blessed Life* (Ventura, CA: Regal, 2004), p. 78.
12. James 2:5.
13. Philippians 4:11–13.
14. John 3:16.
15. 1 John 3:16.
16. 1 Corinthians 12:11; Galatians 5:22–23.
17. 2 Corinthians 9:9.
18. Malachi 3:10.
19. 2 Corinthians 9:7.
20. Exodus 20:17.
21. 1 John 2:15.
22. Isaiah 55:2.
23. Proverbs 22:7; Romans 13:8.
24. Acts 20:35.
25. Psalm 35:27.
26. Proverbs 6:6–8.
27. Proverbs 28:19.
28. Luke 16:11.
29. Compiled by Harry Verplough, *The Quotable Tozer I* (Camp Hills, PA: Christian Publications, 1984), p. 141.
30. Bob Yandian, *From Just Enough to Overflowing* (Tulsa, OK: Albury Publishing, 1996), p. 93.

Chapter 4: Possessions
1. Galatians 3:13–14.
2. Philippians 4:11–13; ESV.
3. Luke 12:15.
4. Arthur G. Gish, *Beyond the Rat Race* (New Canaan, CT: Keats, 1973), p. 21.
5. Martin Luther, Ewald Martin Plass, *What Luther Says: An Anthology* (St. Louis, MO: Concordia Pub. House, 1959), p. 1339
6. Ralph D. Winter, Stephen C. Hawthorne, editors, *Perspectives on the World Christian Movement (Third Edition)* (Pasadena, CA: William Carey Library, 1999), p. 321.

Chapter 5: Rich Advice
1. 1 Timothy 6:17.
2. Proverbs 16:18.
3. James 4:6; 1 Peter 5:5.
4. Psalm 100:3.

5. Proverbs 23:5.
6. 1 Timothy 6:17.
7. Ibid.
8. 1 Timothy 6:18.
9. Ibid.
10. Ibid.
11. Ibid.
12. Matthew 6:19.
13. Harold Myra and Marshall Shelly, *The Leadership Secrets of Billy Graham* (Grand Rapids, MI: Zondervan, 2005), p. 107.

Chapter 6: Rich and Empty
1. Proverbs 8:18.
2. Matthew 6:33.
3. 2 Chronicles 16:9.
4. Dennis Peacocke, *Doing Business God's Way* (Santa Rosa, CA: Rebuild, 2003), p. 57.

Chapter 7: The Covenant Cycle
1. John 1:12; Galatians 3:26.
2. Galatians 3:29.
3. Genesis 12:1–3.
4. Deuteronomy 8:18; NIV.
5. Psalm 67:1.
6. Psalm 67:2.
7. Galatians 3:13–14.
8. Romans 4:5; Galatians 3:29.
9. Ephesians 1:3.
10. John 10:10.
11. Psalm 67:3–7; Matthew 28:19.
12. Isaiah 58:12; NIV.
13. Jack W. Hayford, *The Key to Everything* (Lake Mary, FL: Creation House, 1993), p. 153–154.

Chapter 8: The Money Test
1. Romans 14:10; 1 Corinthians 3:11–15; 2 Corinthians 5:10.
2. 1 Corinthians 3:12–15; NIV.
3. Living Word Missionary Conference, Tulsa, OK, 1995.
4. Genesis 12:1–3.
5. Robert Morris, *The Blessed Life* (Ventura, CA: Regal, 2004), p. 95.

Chapter 9: Why Do the Ungodly Prosper
1. Our only true goodness or righteousness comes from the grace of God. It is God's righteousness imputed to us through faith in Christ. See Romans 3:21–24.
2. Matthew 5:45.
3. Romans 5:12.
4. Acts 17:31.
5. Hebrews 11:25.
6. Galatians 6:7.
7. Ephesians 6:6–8.
8. Psalm 37:1–2.
9. Psalm 92:7.
10. 1 Corinthians 2:9–10.

Chapter 10: Big Business
1. Romans 12:8.
2. See Ed Silvoso, *Anointed for Business* (Ventura, CA: Regal Books, 2002).
3. Matthew 5:14.
4. Matthew 5:15.
5. Matthew 5:16.
6. 1 Corinthians 9:19–23.
7. Philippians 4:19.
8. Robert Morris, *The Blessed Life* (Ventura, CA: Regal Books, 2004), p. 65.
9. Philemon 6; NIV.
10. Matthew 4:19.
11. Matthew 5:16.
12. Romans 1:16.
13. 1 Peter 3:15; NIV.
14. Bill Bright, *As You Sow* (San Bernardino, CA: Here's Life Pub., 1989), p. 16.

Chapter 11: Business by Revelation
1. Luke 5:4.
2. 2 Timothy 3:16.
3. Hebrews 1:1–2.
4. Matthew 4:4.
5. John 14:26.
6. 1 Kings 19:12.
7. Luke 5:5.
8. Luke 5:5.
9. John 15:8.
10. Luke 21:1–13.
11. John 10:27.
12. http://www.worldprayers.org/frameit.cgi?/archive/prayers/invocations/disturb_us_lord_when_we.html. Accessed June 30, 2008.

Chapter 12: Favor
1. 2 Chronicles 16:9.
2. Luke 1:30.
3. Luke 1:28.
4. Luke 1:47.
5. Luke 1:27; NLT.
6. Isaiah 1:18.
7. Luke 1:38.
8. Luke 1:45.
9. Luke 1:46.
10. Luke 1:46–55.
11. Luke 1:48.
12. John 2:5.
13. www.quotationcollection.com/quotation/2360/quote. Accessed June 30, 2008.

Chapter 13: Focus and Follow-through
1. Rick Warren, *God's Answers to Life's Difficult Questions* (Grand Rapids, MI: Zondervan, 2006), p. 18.
2. Philippians 4:13.
3. www.jimcollins.com/lab/hedgehog. Accessed June 30, 2008.
4. Luke 14:28–30.
5. 2 Timothy 4:7.
6. Harold Myra and Marshall Shelley, *The Leadership Secrets of Billy Graham* (Grand Rapids, MI: Zondervan, 2005), p. 65.

Chapter 15: Great Commission Commerce
1. See Ken Eldred, *God Is at Work* (Ventura, CA: Regal Books, 2005).
2. Hebrews 10:24.
3. 2 Timothy 2:2.
4. Nancy Pearcey, *Total Truth* (Wheaton, IL: Crossway Books, 2005), p. 95.

Chapter 16: Healthy Partnerships
1. Deuteronomy 32:30.
2. 2 Corinthians 6:14–15.
3. Proverbs 11:14.
4. Amos 3:3.
5. Ephesians 4:3.

Chapter 17: Hidden Heroes
1. Matthew 5:16.
2. Ephesians 4:28.
3. Matthew 28:19.

Chapter 18: History Lesson
1. John 8:32.
2. 1 Corinthians 10:31.
3. 2 Corinthians 5:17.
4. Matthew 28:19; Mark 16:15.
5. Genesis 1:28.
6. Genesis 1:28.
7. Colossians 1:16–18.
8. Colossians 3:17.
9. Michael Novak, *Business as a Calling* (New York: The Free Press, 1996), p. 37.

Chapter 19: Prayer and the Workplace
1. Joshua 10:12–14.
2. www.oldlandmarks.com/embpow17.htm. Accessed July 1, 2008.
3. Matthew 27:51.
4. John 14:6.
5. Hebrews 10:19–20.
6. Hebrews 4:16.
7. Mrs. Charles Cowman, *Springs in the Valley* (Grand Rapids, MI: Zondervan Pub. House, 1989), p. 216.
8. Matthew 6:7.
9. James 5:16.
10. Matthew 6:9–13.
11. 1 Chronicles 4:10.
12. Acts 4:29–31.
13. John 17:21.
14. Psalm 67:1–2.
15. Zechariah 4:6–7.
16. Psalm 46:10.
17. 1 Corinthians 3:9.
18. Paul E. Billheimer, *Destined for the Throne* (Fort Washington, PA: Christian Literature Crusade, 1975), p. 40.
19. Helen Hosier, compiler, *The Quotable Christian* (Uhrichville, OH: Barbour Publishing, 1998), p. 181.
20. Richard J. Foster, *Celebration of Discipline* (New York: HarperCollins Publishers, 1988), p. 35.

Chapter 20: Prospering from Problems
1. John 16:33.
2. Jeremiah 17:9.
3. Ephesians 6:12.
4. Ephesians 6:13–18.
5. 2 Corinthians 4:17.

6. Galatians 5:22–23.
7. Jeremiah 33:3.

Chapter 21: Right Thinking
1. http://www.quotationpage.com/
   quote/2330.html. Accessed July 1,
   2008.
2. Proverbs 23:7.
3. Romans 12:2; NLT.
4. Lamentations 3:22–23.
5. Revelation 11:15.
6. *The World Book Encyclopedia* (1993)
   Volume E, p. 78.
7. http://www.emdnaz.org/missions_
   prayer_quotes.php. Accessed July 1,
   2008.
8. Proverbs 27:21; NIV.
9. Philippians 4:8.
10. http://www.whymoneymatters.com.
    blogspot/2007/09/youth.html. Ac-
    cessed July 1, 2008.

Chapter 22: Righteous Risk-taking
1. 2 Timothy 1:7.
2. Isaiah 41:10.
3. Zechariah 4:6–7.
4. Hebrews 11:6.
5. Hebrews 11:6.
6. Joshua 1:2.
7. Michael Novak, *Business as a Calling*
   (New York: The Free Press, 1996), p. 32.
8. Psalm 19:13; Matthew 4:7.
9. Matthew 4:5–7.
10. Luke 14:28–30.
11. James 1:5.
12. Proverbs 3:5-6; John 15:4–5.
13. Romans 8:14.
14. David Shibley, *Heaven's Heroes* (Green For-
    est, AR: New Leaf Press, 2004), p. 21.

Chapter 23: Seeds
1. John 15:8.
2. David Shibley, *Challenging Quotes for
   World Changers* (Green Forest, AR:
   New Leaf Press, 1995), p. 38.
3. Betty Lee Skinner, *Daws* (Grand
   Rapids, MI: Zondervan Books, 1974),
   p. 190, 350.
4. Romans 1:14–15.
5. John 12:24.

6. 1 Peter 1:23–25.
7. Galatians 6:6–7.
8. 2 Corinthians 9:10–11.
9. Luke 6:38.
10. Acts 20:35.
11. Proverbs 11:24–25; NIV.
12. John C. Maxwell, *The Success Journey*
    (Nashville, TN: Thomas Nelson,
    1997), p. 11.

Chapter 24: Strong Relationships
1. Luke 6:38.
2. Genesis 1:26–27.
3. John 1:1, 14.
4. John 3:16.
5. Luke 10:27.
6. Acts 9:26–27.
7. Acts 13:1–3.
8. Acts 16:14, 15, 40.
9. Colossians 4:14.
10. Acts 18:1–3, 18.
11. Galatians 2:7, 8, 11; 2 Peter 3:15.

Chapter 25: The Fight of Your Life
1. 1 Corinthians 15:57.
2. 1 John 4:4.
3. 1 Peter 4:12–13.
4. 1 John 1:9.
5. 1 Thessalonians 5:22.
6. Psalm 22:3.
7. Ephesians 5:18; Galatians 5:16.
8. John 15:4.
9. James 4:7.
10. James 5:16.
11. Ephesians 6:11–18.
12. Jude 24–25.
13. Colossians 2:15.
14. 1 Corinthians 10:13.
15. Ephesians 4:27; NLT.
16. 2 Corinthians 5:20.
17. Revelation 12:11; Philippians 4:13.
18. Romans 16:20.
19. Thomas a Kempis, *Of the Imitation of
    Christ*. http://www.ccel.org/k/kempis/
    imitation/formats/imitation-baker.
    html. Accessed July 2, 2008.

Chapter 26: The Ultimate Partnership
1. Dennis Peacocke, *Doing Business God's
   Way* (Santa Rosa, CA: Rebuild, 2003),
   p. 2.

2. Ephesians 2:8.
3. Psalm 24:1.
4. Luke 19:13; NLT.
5. Matthew 9:37.
6. John 4:35.
7. Philippians 3:12.
8. Ephesians 2:10; NIV.
9. http://retirementwithpurpose.com/quotes/quotesgod/html. Accessed July 2, 2008.

Chapter 27: The Weight of Words
1. Richard Reising, *Church Marketing 101* (Grand Rapids, MI: Baker Books, 2005).
2. Proverbs 18:21.
3. James 3:6; NLT.
4. Ephesians 4:29.
5. Numbers 13:25–14:9.
6. Matthew 17:20.
7. Mark 11:23.
8. Revelation 12:10.
9. Psalm 42:5–6; NIV.
10. Joshua 1:8.
11. 2 Corinthians 13:14.
12. John Dawson, "A Word to YWAM," June 1, 2004, International YWAMer.

Chapter 28: The Worth of Your Word
1. Matthew 12:36–37; NIV.
2. Proverbs 22:1.
3. John 14:16–17; 15:26; 16:13.
4. 2 Samuel 12:1–15.
5. Psalm 51:6.
6. James 5:12.
7. Exodus 20:16.

Chapter 29: Thriving under Threat
1. Alan Greenspan, *The Age of Turbulence* (New York: Penguin Press, 2007).
2. Tom Peters, *Thriving on Chaos* (New York: Harper Books, 1988).
3. Matthew 24:6.
4. Acts 20:24.
5. Galatians 2:20.
6. Mark 8:35; NLT.
7. Acts 20:24.
8. 2 Timothy 4:7.
9. Philippians 3:1; NIV.
10. Galatians 5:22.

11. Esther 4:13–14.
12. Southwestern Baptist Theological Seminary chapel service, 1979.

Chapter 30: Dealing with Disaster
1. Romans 5:5; KJV.
2. Romans 12:15.
3. Matthew 5:16.
4. John 9:1–3.
5. John 10:10.
6. Luke 13:4–5.
7. Romans 8:22.
8. 2 Peter 3:13.
9. Matthew 24:7; NLT.
10. Amos 4:12.
11. A.W. Tozer, *The Pursuit of God* (Chapel Hill, PA: Christian Publications, 1993), p. 28.

Chapter 31: Our Work as Worship
1. Proverbs 10:4; NIV.
2. Colossians 3:23; NIV.
3. Deuteronomy 5:13–14.
4. Ephesians 2:10.
5. John 4:34, 9:4.
6. John 17:4.
7. Matthew 9:38.
8. Matthew 6:3–4.
9. Colossians 3:17.
10. 1 Peter 4:10–11.
11. Revelation 14:13.
12. Oswald Chambers, *My Utmost for His Highest* (Uhrichsville, OH: Barbour Publishing, n.d.), p. 32.
13. John Piper, "Why God Wills Work," sermon, September 4, 1983, Bethlehem Baptist Church, Minneapolis, MN.

Chapter 32: Your Competitive Advantage
1. John 10:10.
2. 2 Chronicles 16:9.
3. 1 Chronicles 4:10.
4. Psalm 5:12.
5. Colossians 1:16–17.
6. John 15:4–5.
7. Psalm 119:105.
8. Galatians 5:22–23.
9. Romans 12:1–2; Hebrews 5:14.
10. James 4:8.

Chapter 33: Your Marketplace Mission

1. Matthew 28:19; Mark 16: 15.
2. Genesis 1:28.
3. Matthew 5:13.
4. Matthew 5:14.
5. Abraham Kuyper, "Sovereignty in Its Own Circle," inaugural lecture of the Free University of Amsterdam, October 20, 1880.
6. 2 Corinthians 5:20.

Chapter 34: A Multigenerational Mindset

1. Edmund Burke, *Select Works of Edmund Burke, Vol. 2,* http://www.econlib.org/library/LFBooks/Burke/brkSWv2c0.html. Accessed July 3, 2008.
2. Philippians 1:6.
3. 2 Corinthians 5:17.
4. David Shibley, *Living as if Heaven Matters* (Lake Mary, FL: Charisma House, 2007), p. 15–16.
5. 2 Timothy 2:2.
6. Philippians 1:27.
7. Howard Hendricks, "A Mandate for Mentoring.," Promise Keepers Message, 1993.

Chapter 35: Bottom Line Passion

1. Isaiah 9:7, NLT.
2. William P. Merrill, "Rise Up, O Men of God" (1911).
3. Quoted in David Shibley, *The Missions Addiction* (Lake Mary, FL: Charisma House, 2001), p. 6.
4. Isaiah 6:8.
5. Psalm 57:11; NIV.
6. 3 John 1:7; NIV.
7. Psalm 67:5; NIV.
8. Romans 15:16; NIV.
9. Revelation 5:12.
10. Charles Wesley, "O for a Thousand Tongues to Sing" (1739).
11. Dietrich Bonhoeffer, *The Cost of Discipleship* (New York: Macmillan Books, 1970), p. 196.
12. Quoted in Elisabeth Elliot, *Shadow of the Almighty* (New York: Harper & Brothers, 1958), p. 249.

Chapter 36: Integrity

1. http://www.worldofquotes.com/topic/Character/1/index.html. Accessed July 3, 2008.
2. http://www.pbs.org/newshour/character/quotes/ Accessed July 3, 2008.
3. James 4:10; 1 Peter 5:6.
4. James 4:6; 1 Peter 5:5.
5. Quoted in Harold Myra and Marshall Shelly, *The Leadership Secrets of Billy Graham* (Grand Rapids, MI: Zondervan, 2005), p. 198.
6. Mark 10:42–43; NLT.
7. Andrew Murray, *Humility* (Gainesville, FL: Bridge-Logos Publishers, 2000), p. 94.
8. Proverbs 27:17; NIV.
9. Psalm 119:9; NIV.
10. Hebrews 12:5–7.
11. Romans 8:29; Philippians 1:6.
12. Hebrews 12:10.
13. Frontline Shepherds Conference, Amman, Jordon, April 2005.
14. 1 John 1:9.
15. Song of Songs 2:15; NIV.
16. Proverbs 22:1.
17. 2 Corinthians 5:10.
18. Quoted by Harold Myra and Marshall Shelly, *The Leadership Secrets of Billy Graham* (Grand Rapids, MI: Zondervan, 2005), p. 60.

Chapter 37: Your Greatest Asset

1. John Brown University Press Release, "Center for Relationship Enrichment Responds to Study, Offers Help for NWA" April 16, 2008.
2. Ephesians 5:25.
3. Ephesians 5:25–28.
4. Proverbs 24:30–34, NLT.
5. 1 Corinthians 6:19–20.
6. 1 Thessalonians 4:3–8.
7. Romans 12:1–2.
8. Revelation 2:2–5.
9. http://www.impactsolutions.us/marriage.htm. Accessed July 3, 2008.

Chapter 38: Your Unique Contribution

1. Philippians 3:12.

2. Jeff McLoud, *Achieving Authentic Wealth* (Roanoke, TX: Guy Thing Press, 2007), p. 66.

3. Winston S. Churchill, *The Second World War: Volume I, The Gathering Storm* (Boston, MA: Houghton Mifflin Company, 1949), p. 666–667.

4. Jeremiah 1:5.

5. Os Guinness, *The Call: Finding and Fulfilling the Central Purpose of Your Life* (Nashville, TN: Word Publishing, 1988), p. 29.

6. Insights from this chapter were first published in David Shibley, "Hitting Your Ministry Sweet Spot," *Ministry Today* (July–August 2008): p. 47–50. Used by permission.

7. Ed Silvoso, *Anointed for Business: How Christians Can Use Their Influence in the Marketplace to Change the World* (Ventura, CA: Regal Books, 2002).

8. Romans 12:3–8; 1 Corinthians 12:4–11; Ephesians 4:11.

9. 2 Timothy 1:6.

10. 1 Corinthians 9:16.

11. John Piper, *Don't Waste Your Life* (Wheaton, IL: Crossway Books, 2003), p. 47.

Chapter 39: Leave a Legacy

1. John 19:5.

2. Russell Kirk, *Edmund Burke: A Genius Reconsidered* (New Rochelle, NY: Arlington House, 1967), p. 510.

3. Proverbs 10:7.

4. Exodus 34:7.

5. Proverbs 22:4; NIV.

6. Proverbs 14:26; NIV.

7. John 15:8.

8. Luke 22:31.

9. Charles R. Swindoll, *So You Want to Be Like Christ?* (Nashville, TN: Thomas Nelson, 2005), p. 138.

10. 2 Corinthians 2:15–16.

11. Matthew 25:21; Matthew 25:23.

12. Adapted from David Shibley, *Living as if Heaven Matters* (Lake Mary, FL: Charisma House, 2007), p. 161.